LAUNCHING LBJ

LAUNCHING LBJ

*How a Kennedy Insider Helped
Define Johnson's Presidency*

HELEN O'DONNELL

Skyhorse Publishing

Skyhorse Publishing books may be purchased in bulk at special discounts for sales promotion, corporate gifts, fund-raising, or educational purposes. Special editions can also be created to specifications. For details, contact the Special Sales Department, Skyhorse Publishing, 307 West 36th Street, 11th Floor, New York, NY 10018 or info@skyhorsepublishing.com.

Skyhorse® and Skyhorse Publishing® are registered trademarks of Skyhorse Publishing, Inc.®, a Delaware corporation.

Visit our website at www.skyhorsepublishing.com.

10 9 8 7 6 5 4 3 2 1

Library of Congress Cataloging-in-Publication Data is available on file.

Cover design by Rain Saukas
Cover photo credit: AP Photo

ISBN: 978-1-5107-1700-8
Ebook ISBN: 978-1-5107-1701-5

Printed in the United States of America

For
Kathy & Tom Schlichenmaier
and
Jason, Allison, Erin & Jack

CONTENTS

Introduction   xi

Chapter One: A Call from Bobby   1
Chapter Two: Mr. Leader   7
Chapter Three: The Bathroom at the Biltmore   13
Chapter Four: The Exercise of Power   27
Chapter Five: Dallas, Texas, November 22, 1963   42
Chapter Six: The Long Journey Home   50
Chapter Seven: The Transition   77
Chapter Eight: Making Them All "Johnson Men"   85
Chapter Nine: Emancipation   94
Chapter Ten: The Johnson Style   110
Chapter Eleven: "I've Got Me a Bobby Problem"   119
Chapter Twelve: Hardball Politics   134
Chapter Thirteen: The President   146
Chapter Fourteen: The Campaign   157
Chapter Fifteen: The Anti-Campaign   167
Chapter Sixteen: Victory   180
Chapter Seventeen: On Their Own   193

Epilogue   205
Acknowledgments   211
Sources   214

"Change is the law of life. And those who look only to the past or present are certain to miss the future."
—John F. Kennedy

INTRODUCTION

On November 22, 1963, my father, Kenneth P. O'Donnell, had his world shattered. My dad was one of the most powerful people in the United States government, due in large measure to the trust and friendship placed in him by the thirty-fifth president President of the United States, John F. Kennedy. And yet, he couldn't save his friend and president.

In Dallas, Texas, on that day, the nation and the world witnessed the murder of Jack Kennedy. Jackie Kennedy and her children lost a husband and father. Bobby Kennedy lost his beloved, idolized older brother. My dad saw his president, his friend, and his hope for the future destroyed in a shattering crack of gunfire.

And that might well have been the end of the story, but for one man—a man who needed Kenny O'Donnell as much as Kenny needed to have a mission. Lyndon Baines Johnson became an unlikely hero not only for my father, but for the legacy of John F. Kennedy and, in the end, for the country.

This book is the untold story, from my father's point of view and from taped recollections of the journey from Dealey Plaza in 1963 to Washington, DC, in November of 1964.

This is the story of Ken O'Donnell's journey after Jack Kennedy's murder, the story of how Kenny and Lyndon Johnson became unlikely allies and, indeed, unlikely friends for a critical period of time, and who together became determined, for different reasons perhaps, to fulfill the final legacy of John F. Kennedy. In so doing, Johnson found his voice as president and O'Donnell fulfilled a legacy he could not have done otherwise.

For a brief interlude, later interrupted by outside events and differing personal choices, this is the story of two men joining forces to finish the work begun by Jack Kennedy.

In so doing, they changed the course of American history and altered the very fabric of American society for the better.

CHAPTER ONE
A CALL FROM BOBBY

"Bobby Kennedy was my best pal from Harvard," Kenny recalled years later. "I had gone to work for his older brother John Kennedy in 1952. Bobby and I worked on John Kennedy's run for United States senator. We won! It was no small victory for us. We were outsiders and we took on the Democratic establishment and licked 'em. The plan had been for me to stay in Massachusetts and help build the political machinery that would eventually get then Senator Kennedy elected to the White House."

That might have been where Kenny stayed, but for an interruption in the form of a telephone call from his pal Bobby Kennedy, then in Washington, DC, working for the irascible Senator John McClellan, senior senator from the state of Arkansas. Bobby was chief counsel for the Senate Select Committee on Improper Activities in the Labor or Management Field, which was dubbed by the press the "Rackets Committee." The purpose of the committee was to pursue organized crime infiltration in the labor unions. This was a tough gig if your older brother was a Democrat who hoped to be president with the help of the same labor unions.

Bobby was a single-minded, relentless prosecutor, which didn't help things very much. John Kennedy had agreed to serve on the committee with his brother, but at the moment it wasn't going very well.

Still, none of that involved Kenny O'Donnell, who, along with his so-called "Irish Mafia" pal Larry O'Brien, was up in the Kennedy office in Boston happily chasing down votes and securing political power for Jack Kennedy's future political plans in Massachusetts. That was until the shrill ring of the telephone late one evening in the small living room of the O'Donnell home in the seaside town of Winthrop, Massachusetts, a blue-collar, working-class suburb just across the bay from Boston.

John Kennedy was then happily in Washington, DC, as the newly elected senator from Massachusetts, having been one of the few Democrats to overcome the Eisenhower political tide in that year's presidential contest. Kenny and Larry O'Brien were at the state Democratic headquarters when Bobby first called. Kenny presumed he was calling for Jack on political business, but it turned out to be something else entirely.

"Bobby had this crazy idea that I should come down to Washington and work with him on his subcommittee. I said no. But Bobby can be a pain in the ass sometimes. He doesn't take no very well, if at all," Kenny said.

Bobby explained to Kenny that he had just begun this investigation. He thought it was sort of a minor thing when it began, but suddenly it had gotten blown out of proportion with Teamsters head Dave Beck involved in some deep, dark waters that could potentially involve a fellow named Jimmy Hoffa and the mob. Bobby told Kenny he needed him down in Washington. "I need someone down here to give me some protection and have my back. Someone who is a friend, someone I can trust to watch my back. I need you," Bobby explained.

Kenny remained unmoved. While he knew in general terms who Dave Beck was, he had only a remote sense of this guy Hoffa and he couldn't quite grasp the "mob" angle. He made it plain to Bobby he was happy doing what he was doing, and so he told Bobby it was, as Kenny remembered it, "a flat out no." Bobby was not easily deterred. Undaunted, he picked up the telephone to Kenny's wife Helen and they began to hatch a plan.

Reddish-blonde with sparkling blue eyes, an athletic build, and a wicked sense of humor, Helen was a good balance for Kenny, who could be intimidating and taciturn to those who didn't know him well. Helen and Bobby had become, as she put it, "great pals" going back to their first meeting at Harvard. So it was no surprise that Bobby enlisted her help to get Kenny to change his mind.

The following week, Kenny and Helen were just sitting for a drink and a chance to catch up on the day's events. She had put the last of their three children to bed and was looking forward to this evening ritual with her husband. He poured each of them a drink and lit her cigarette. While Kenny never smoked, his wife loved Pall Malls each evening with her cocktail. Kenny had just begun to tell her of their efforts on Jack's behalf with the committee, when the ring of the black phone broke into their conversation. Not wanting the children to wake up at this late hour, Helen jumped up and grabbed it. Kenny stood and refreshed his drink while he listened to Helen's happy chatter. Before he even took the telephone he knew it was Bobby. There had been enough references to Washington, Ethel, and babies on the way that when he heard Bobby's voice, he could skip the preliminaries. He knew Bobby well enough to know he would not call at this hour without a reason.

"What's up now?" he asked.

"I need you to come to Washington and work with me on

the committee. I need someone who has my back. Someone I can trust. The work is dangerous and I need your help," Bobby said, almost as if he had not heard Kenny's answer the week previous. "Kenny, I cannot take no for an answer. You asked me to give up my life in Washington to come run Jack's campaign in 1952. I didn't want to do it, but I did it because you are my friend and you needed my help. Now I need you to return the favor."

Bobby was direct, no nonsense, and the two friends sat in silence over the long-distance line for just a moment.

Kenny was dismayed. He had no interest in moving to Washington to work for the Rackets Committee. In fact, he had no interest in government work at all. Politics was where he wanted to be.

"Look, Bobby," Kenny began, "I don't want to go. I like what I am doing for your brother. I love the political front. We've got to focus on 1958 and running up some big numbers. What the hell do I know about the mob and the labor unions?"

But Bobby wasn't having it. "I need you," he repeated. Then Bobby quickly ticked off two areas that he thought would convince Kenny to say yes. "Look," Bobby said, "it is a nice paycheck and benefits, neither of which you are getting now. Secondly, it is fine with Jack. It is temporary and when we are done you can go back to Boston and resume your political work."

The paycheck was immediately appealing. At the moment Kenny was working as an unpaid political consultant for Jack Kennedy. It was not that Jack Kennedy had not tried to get Kenny on either the Senate staff or the payroll from the Kennedy family in New York, it was just that Kenny had flat out refused. It had been a calculated decision on Kenny's part to assure his independence and it was a move that impressed both Jack Kennedy and his father, Joe (who actually controlled the purse strings). While the Kennedys may have been impressed, and it certainly assured Kenny's long-term role and garnered great respect from Jack Kennedy, the move had not made Helen too happy.

She had complained bitterly about the situation to Bobby when he had made his trips to Boston and the Cape to go watch football games with Kenny and visit his dad at the compound. Kenny's long-term strategic move, while good politics with the Kennedys, had made the O'Donnell family completely dependent on Helen's small salary as a secretary in a job she loathed and was eager to quit.

"I didn't want to be paid by the Kennedy family or the Senate," Kenny explained. "My grandfather knew old Joe Kennedy very well. They had gone to Boston Latin School together. I knew from my father's stories and what I had seen in person that if the Kennedys pay you, they think they own you. Like most rich people, they then see you differently, almost beneath them, because you need their money. I knew by making the decision I made that Senator John Kennedy and I would always remain equals. It was worth the sacrifice and would pay off in the end." All of that was certainly true, but it didn't make anything easier in 1956 as the O'Donnells tried to make ends meet.

So when Bobby called he knew where to focus his argument. His first approach was the nice paycheck. "It would be coming from the United States government, not me," Bobby said, "so that should address your concern there." While Bobby made the economic argument, he made sure never to tell Kenny that he and Helen had already discussed all this ahead of time.

"Well, that's good," Kenny said, "but what about your brother?" Kenny was still hoping for a way to say no.

But Bobby then told him that "the senator was fine with it."

"So I sort of presumed that the brothers had spoken to each other and that this was all cleared with John Kennedy. Well, it had not been, and he was not too happy a fellow when he saw me in Washington," Kenny recalled later.

"I never exactly said I had talked to Jack—I indicated I would," Bobby later explained with a laugh. But John Kennedy was furious. Kenny learned a critical and valuable lesson for the future and that was never to do anything that you had not spoken to Senator Kennedy about first. "I learned never to be so stupid as to presume anything with him again."

An angry John Kennedy told Kenny in no uncertain terms that he had planned for Kenny to run his 1958 campaign for Senate, not "work as some damn clerk for Bobby. You are my friend and you work for me, not Bobby."

By now it was too late; Helen—with Bobby's help—had secured a house to rent. Everyone was moving or already moved. There was no going back. "The senator and I realized we had been hoodwinked by Bobby and my wife, but it was done now, so we made some accommodations. It was decided as soon as Bobby was out of danger and the situation was stable, I would head back up to Boston and run the campaign. My family would stay here and I would just live at the Kennedy family apartment at 122 Bowdoin Street in Boston across from the State House. I will say, stabilizing the situation took a great deal longer and was much more complicated and dangerous than either the senator or I had first imagined. But I never made a decision without talking with him directly again," Kenny recalled. "It was my move to Washington that brought about my first, albeit brief and not too pleasant, encounter with the majority leader—one Lyndon Baines Johnson."

CHAPTER TWO
MR. LEADER

Bobby's office was Room 130 in the old Senate office building. It was the office for the Senate Select Committee on Improper Activities in the Labor or Management Field. It was a small cramped space where every desk was stacked with papers, the telephones never stopped ringing, and there was a constant, thunderous clack of the typewriters. As they walked in for the first time, Bobby told Kenny it was "controlled chaos."

Kenny gave Bobby a disdainful stare and said, "No, Bobby, this is just chaos, there is nothing controlled about it." Angie Novello, Bobby's secretary—who would stay with him all the way to Los Angeles in 1968—said of Kenny's arrival: "He was like Moses parting the Red Sea. When he arrived, suddenly everything fell into place and began to make sense. We knew what we had to do. His arrival was exactly what Bobby needed at that moment. He needed someone to have his back. We all did. Kenny made the trains run on time."

Kenny said the first encounter that he and Bobby had with then Majority Leader Lyndon Baines Johnson was less than successful. It certainly had been unintentional, but looking back years later, Kenny said the encounter seemed to set the tone for the relationship between Lyndon and Bobby.

Hearings for the committee had been scheduled for the Senate hearing room where they were usually held. But this particular hearing featured more witnesses than usual, so Bobby had ordered it moved to a room usually reserved for the majority leader. The hearing room was large, well-situated, and grander than the one they usually used. One didn't schedule use of the room unless it was cleared through the majority leader's office. And that could only be done by another senator. In this case it would have to have been scheduled by the chairman of Bobby's committee, Senator John McClellan of Arkansas. The majority leader was a Senate man and thus a strict believer in the Senate rules, codes of behavior, and especially seniority.

"Bobby never bothered much about that kind of thing," Kenny later explained. Pierre Salinger, a member of the committee and eventual press secretary to John Kennedy, put it another way: "Bobby was about action. He would never waste his time checking off boxes to make sure somebody was not offended. If he wanted something done, he would do it. He would worry about the consequences later."

The day of the hearing arrived and with everyone seated and ready to proceed, including members of the press who covered labor issues as their beat, such as intrepid reporter Clark Mollenhoff. In fact, it was Mollenhoff who had convinced Bobby to look into the Teamsters Union. Senator McClellan had just gaveled the hearing to order when Johnson's top aide, Bobby Baker, arrived. Baker whispered something to McClellan, who went ashen and "suddenly the hearing was postponed and we were kicked out," Kenny said with a laugh. "Lyndon had not even needed to use the hearing room that morning, but he kicked us out anyway, just to remind McClellan—and, as it turned out, Bobby—just who was in charge."

About an hour later, Kenny and Bobby were called to Johnson's spacious office in the Capitol. There stood McClellan chomping on a cigar, drink in hand, eyeing Bobby with annoyance. It was clear that Senator McClellan was looking for an apology from Bobby to Johnson.

Johnson was standing there, leaning against the desk in a suit that seemed almost too big for him. Nevertheless, he exuded power without saying a word. Senator McClellan introduced Bobby and Kenny by saying, "these two are the young men who made the scheduling mistake." Kenny laughed as he remembered the conversation: "Typical of McClellan. He had no trouble throwing us under the bus in order to stay on Johnson's good side."

Johnson stood, arms folded. "You are Joe Kennedy's boy, aren't you?" he asked. According to Kenny, Bobby bristled visibly and took a step back even as he extended his hand. He hated being spoken of as his father's son. Bobby would spend his life battling to get out from under the shadow of his father and brother.

"Yes," was all Bobby managed in response. Bobby had resented being pulled away from his office for this silly meeting. As a result, he was sullen and withdrawn. Senator McClellan then introduced Kenny to Johnson by way of Harvard and his friendship with Bobby. Kenny quickly corrected him by saying he was from Worcester, Massachusetts, a blue-collar working town. His father was a football coach at Holy Cross College. After a few moments of football talk, he and Bobby left. Kenny teased Bobby that he never did apologize to the majority leader. Bobby shrugged it off. "I am too busy to worry about such stuff," he told Kenny.

Kenny laughed. "I don't think we had one more encounter with Lyndon the entire time we were there at the committee. I would say that Lyndon thought of Bobby and I as a couple of young, wet-behind-the-ears kids, and he likely never gave us another thought until 1956 in Chicago. Of course the truth was, he was correct about us. We knew nothing at the time. The truth was that he only dealt with Robert Kennedy and myself in a very cursory manner. If Bobby dealt with him much at all it was a very cursory fashion at this stage. If the majority leader, the most powerful man in the Senate, was going to deal with anyone, it would be Senator McClellan, who he would consider his contemporary. Not a couple of staff members."

There may have been some truth to that, but others heard something different: that Johnson was to have said he had heard good things about Bobby—that he was smart, bright, and going places. But he is quoted as saying, "The kid could use some lessons in good manners."

At the Democratic convention in 1956, Jack Kennedy very nearly ended up as the vice president to Adlai Stevenson. But in a move that Johnson called "the goddamnedest, stupidest move a politician could make," Stevenson decided on an open convention. Despite warnings from his father to stay out of the race for the vice presidency, Jack jumped into the fray anyway. Kenny recalled, "Bobby and I didn't know a soul. We ran around that convention floor like a couple of nuts. We got nowhere. Johnson, on the other hand, following the wise advice from Mr. Sam (Rayburn), watched the chaos from afar."

Once Jack saw the political writing on the wall and saw the delegates' overwhelmingly positive reaction to him during his concession speech, he knew he'd been damn lucky to have avoided the vice-presidential spot. He also knew that Stevenson had come off as boring, gray, and old news. Sure, maybe Jack had lost, but as he had in the lead-up to the Massachusetts Senate race in 1952, he told Kenny and Bobby that he intended to turn this loss to his advantage, and that it set him on the road to 1960.

In later years, when Jack and Kenny would sit around the White House, winding down after a stressful day, Jack would upon occasion reflect on events, both planned and unplanned, that brought them to this moment in his career.

Kenny said to Jack, "Losing that vice-presidential nomination in 1956 was the best thing that ever happened to you. Without it, you would never have won in 1960."

Jack laughed. "Fate," he said, "is a funny thing."

It was only later that the significance of the moment became clear.

"You would think we'd have known that," Kenny remarked later. "But in the moment of it we got very caught up in it. We never made that mistake again. Though our instincts were wrong, as I said before, it backfired beautifully for 1960, but certainly not because we planned it that way. That is the beautiful thing about politics. It is always unpredictable."

And so the stage was set for Bobby's and Johnson's next encounter, which would not go much better. That would be the battle for the vice-presidential nomination in 1956. The problem for Johnson as 1956 approached was, as Kenny put it, "[he] was unable to fully escape the fiercely competitive struggle of Texas politics." "Thus," Rowland Evans reported, "Johnson's entry into national Democratic politics in 1956 would hardly be a success. Following his failure in Chicago and watching Kennedy wisely side-step a near disaster, Johnson returned to Washington a wiser man, armed by the failure of 1956 and like Kennedy eyeing the more glittering opportunity of 1960. But, paradoxically, instead of profiting from the lessons of 1956, as Kennedy had, Johnson would demonstrate that he still could not master the realities of national Democratic politics. The truth was, if 1956 was a disappointment to Johnson, 1960 was to approach disaster."

Kenny maintained that despite Johnson's half-hearted efforts in 1956, Johnson was not considered a contender:

> The truth is, up until 1958, there was no real serious effort on Lyndon's behalf. He had had that serious heart attack, which immobilized him for a time. I think after the 1956 convention it became obvious that John Kennedy was going to be a serious contender. In 1958 we were running our campaign up in Massachusetts and we paid no attention to Lyndon Johnson. We never considered him as a serious candidate for 1960 and I speak for myself and then-Senator Kennedy. We felt that the majority leader and Speaker Sam Rayburn were too conservative for us and they represented the past. We felt that from a political point of view they were overly cooperative with President Eisenhower. We accepted them from a philosophical sense as southern leadership, which was different than ours at that time. But it was certainly nothing personal. None of us ever considered Lyndon Johnson as a formal contender at that time. He was not well himself, and whether he would ever get back on his feet and certainly get back to be a candidate for president was unthinkable to us. We had made a very cold analysis that a southerner could not be elected president at that time under any circumstances, and so therefore we didn't consider it. As for Bobby, I never heard him mention Lyndon again until Los Angeles in July 1960.

In the end, only one man could emerge victorious, and how that happened would come down to a bathroom at the Biltmore Hotel in Los Angeles, California, in July 1960.

CHAPTER THREE

THE BATHROOM AT THE BILTMORE

As the Kennedy presidential campaign began 1959 by gearing up for a fight for the Democratic nomination, Lyndon was simply not on the radar screen. As Jack, Bobby, Kenny, Larry, Ted Sorenson, Pierre Salinger, and others sat at the Kennedy family estate at Palm Beach, they considered their most viable possible opponents; Lyndon Johnson simply didn't make the list.

"In 1959 and 1960," Kenny recalled, "Lyndon was recuperating [from a heart attack] . . . and it became a little more evident that despite everything else and his health, he might be a candidate. But we still considered the chance remote. In 1959 I think we thought that if there was going to be any serious opposition, it probably was going to be Senator Stuart Symington from Missouri, who had already gotten the support of former President Truman. Frankly, we felt he would be difficult."

Kenny and Dave Powers arrived in Los Angeles a week before the convention. Dave Powers was perhaps one of Jack Kennedy's closest friends. He had begun with Kennedy in his first race for Congress in 1946. Powers understood Boston politics as well as anybody at that time. He also possessed an easy manner, loyalty, and a keen Irish wit that made him indispensable to Jack.

In Los Angeles, the plan was to locate a hideaway apartment where Jack could rest and recuperate away from prying eyes. The location was 522 North Rossmore in the Hancock Park district of Los Angeles. The private three-bedroom penthouse belonged to the actor Jack Haley and his wife, Flo. The quiet white and pink stucco building was ideal for Jack Kennedy—it featured a private entrance with an elevator that brought him straight to his apartment.

For purposes of public consumption and political strategy, they had also taken a suite of rooms at the Biltmore Hotel in downtown Los Angeles. The Kennedy suite, 8315, was just a few floors above where Lyndon Johnson and Speaker Rayburn had taken rooms. Jack decided to stay at the apartment for the first four or five nights of the convention, leaving every morning in a car equipped with a telephone in order to keep the candidate in constant communication with Bobby, his brother-in-law Steve Smith, and Kenny, who was down at the convention site.

"There were, thankfully, no real problems," Kenny said. "After our experience in 1956 we had the convention pretty much buttoned up, but the senator began to get increasingly annoyed with Adlai Stevenson's refusal to come to his support." On behalf of Senator Kennedy, Kenny and Bobby tried one last time to get Stevenson to give the nominating speech for Jack, just as Jack had done for him in Chicago in 1956. But Stevenson still clung to hope of a miracle that would give him—Stevenson—the nomination. With that in mind, he continued to insist he had to remain neutral.

"Look Kenny," Adlai explained, "I must remain neutral.

Just in case it is necessary and something happens." Bobby was disgusted. "We have it locked, Adlai," Bobby snapped. "Nothing is going to happen to give you the nomination."

Kenny, realizing the situation was pointless, dragged an exhausted Bobby away from the meeting before things could get uglier.

"Neutral my ass!" exclaimed a frustrated John Kennedy when Kenny and Bobby informed him of their failed attempt to persuade Stevenson. "You mean he is neutral for Johnson! He has a short memory. He's forgetting that I was with him in '56 when Johnson and Rayburn were both against him."

Despite the hopes of both Stevenson and Johnson, the Kennedy team had the nomination largely wrapped up, and on Wednesday, July 13, 1960, John Kennedy and his "Irish Brotherhood," led by Bobby, Kenny, Larry, Ted Sorenson, and Pierre Salinger, celebrated the nomination once they heard youngest Kennedy brother, Teddy, call out the count from the Wyoming delegation. As Bobby confirmed later, "Up until that point there had been no serious consideration of the vice-presidential slot." Kenny put it this way: "John Kennedy was not a fellow who would count on something before it happened. He never was sure he had the nomination until he had the nomination. He was not the type of fellow to discuss the number two spot before he had won the thing."

Jack Kennedy did not give any serious consideration to the number two spot until after he returned to the North Rossmore apartment the evening of the nomination. Both Kenny and Bobby were clear on that point. "Before that moment he was completely concerned with rounding up delegates to support him in the presidential balloting. But over the earlier months of countrywide campaigning, the choice of the second name on the ticket seemed far from his mind," Kenny reported. Bobby confirmed that he knew for a fact that the week of his arrival in Los Angeles, his brother had told him he had "made no promises or definite offers to anybody."

Kenny was clear, too, when he said later: "We knew that Lyndon Johnson was on his list of possible vice presidents, but none of us ever thought that Jack Kennedy would pick Johnson, whom he regarded as a conservative Old Guardsman opposed to the moderate liberalism of John Kennedy."

In fact, both Bobby and Kenny were so sure that Lyndon Johnson had no chance at the vice presidency that, in a move that would come back to haunt them later, they both gave their word and personal assurances to the labor people that Johnson would have "no shot at the number two slot." "I gave my word to the labor guys," Kenny said, "who were critical both to our winning the nomination, as well as winning in November. Well, I gave my word on behalf of Jack Kennedy that Lyndon Johnson was not under consideration. Afterwards, when all hell broke loose, I realized I shouldn't have gone that far in promises and assurances to the labor people. But I have to admit both Bobby and I were as surprised as anyone. Hell, I think even Lyndon Johnson was surprised."

When Jack came back to the apartment after visiting the convention on the night of his nomination, he celebrated with Ann Gargan, Evelyn Lincoln, Torby MacDonald, and a few other people who were waiting to greet him. Evelyn played "When Irish Eyes Are Smiling" on the piano. Jack said to Dave Powers, "I'll have that beer now, Dave." When Dave poured the beer, the first alcoholic drink accepted by Kennedy that day, the group drank a toast to the party's new standard bearer. Then Jack ate his victory supper, two eggs fried in butter and served with toast, jelly, and milk. Jack looked at a few of the congratulatory telegrams that had been received at the apartment and read aloud a warm and cordial message from Lyndon Johnson. After the guests had left, Kennedy sat at the kitchen table drinking his second glass of milk and read again to Dave one of the lines in Johnson's telegram: "LBJ now stands for Let's Back Jack."

The telegram apparently got Jack thinking, and though it was two o'clock in the morning on the West Coast, Jack asked Dave to put a call in to Johnson right then. A sleepy aide told Dave that Johnson was in bed and could not be disturbed. Jack then had Dave call Evelyn Lincoln, who had a room at the Biltmore. Since Evelyn had just left the apartment only a few moments before, she had not yet reached her hotel room. The call woke her husband, Abe. Jack took the phone from Dave and dictated a message to Johnson, which Abe typed on Evelyn's portable typewriter. He then instructed Abe to hand-deliver the message to Johnson's suite. The message said that Kennedy wanted to see Johnson at ten o'clock tomorrow morning in suite 8315 of the Biltmore.

Once that was done Jack headed for bed, but not before telling Dave to "set the alarm early. I want to be up by 7:15. I wish I had asked Lyndon and George Smathers to be at that meeting of southern governors we've got scheduled for 11:30."

As Dave climbed exhausted into his own bed later that night, he thought, "My God, he is going to offer it to Lyndon Johnson!"

The next morning, Jack woke bright and early. On his first day as the Democratic nominee for president, he enjoyed his usual eggs, bacon, coffee, juice, and milk prepared by Dave. They then headed up to the Biltmore Hotel and suite 8315. As he walked into the suite and picked up his messages and more congratulatory telegrams from Evelyn Lincoln, he asked her to call Johnson's suite and see if he was up yet. At about that moment Bobby arrived. He had gotten some sleep, but still looked tired and disheveled with his tie pulled down, no suit coat, and his shirt out of his pants. Jack briefly teased his brother about his attire before asking him to follow him into the bedroom. Once inside the brothers closed the door. After about twenty minutes they emerged.

Bobby looked resigned. He told Kenny later he was too tired to argue about it. "I really think it is Jack's decision to make in any manner he wishes to do so," Bobby said. Kenny told him he could not disagree more.

All Dave heard Bobby say was, "If you're sure that's what you want to do, then go ahead and see him."

Later, Dave said to Kenny that he was surprised that Bobby would take the news so calmly, but it was then that he realized that whatever Jack wanted to do was okay with Bobby. Dave joked to Kenny, "If Jack had said, I want Eleanor Roosevelt as vice president, it would have been alright with Bobby."

The first Kenny realized what was happening was when Pierre Salinger called Kenny in his room and asked him to come to Bobby's suite, which was on the floor below Jack's. When Kenny walked in, he thought Pierre looked "glum."

"You do remember we won, Pierre, right? What could possibly be wrong?" Kenny asked, as he poured himself a coffee.

Pierre heaved a sigh before helping himself to a coffee as well. "Bobby just asked me to add up the electoral states we are sure of and to add Texas."

Kenny couldn't believe it. Slamming his cup down, he said, "You must be kidding." Pierre shook his head. "I wish I was," he replied.

"Where is he?" Pierre nodded his head towards the closed bathroom door. Kenny stormed into the bathroom, where Bobby was sitting in the steaming bath with his eyes closed, a yellow pad and paper with the electoral count by state beside the tub. Bobby opened his eyes and, seeing the fury in Kenny's face, visibly winced and sighed.

"Don't worry about the closed door," Bobby quipped, trying unsuccessfully for some humor.

"Don't tell me it's Johnson," Kenny snapped.

Bobby sighed again. "I guess it is. He is seeing him now."

Kenny was so furious that he could hardly talk. "Do you realize this is a disaster, Bobby? Nixon will love this. Now Nixon can say Kennedy is just another phony politician who will say anything to get elected. I want to talk to your brother myself on this one."

Bobby heaved a sigh and stood up as Kenny handed him a towel. "All right. All right. As soon as I get dressed we will go up and see him."

As Kenny recalled later: "I thought of all the promises I had made to the labor leaders and the civil rights groups, the assurances we had given that Johnson would not be on the ticket if Kennedy was the nominee. I felt we had been double-crossed."

The Kennedy suite was filled with throngs of northern Democratic leaders. "Dave Lawrence, who had given Kennedy nothing but trouble, was acting as if the Johnson selection was all his idea. I just stared at him and was about ready to slug him when Jack, seeing the look on my face, pulled himself away from Ohio's governor Mike DiSalle and signaled I should follow him," Kenny explained. "When Jack saw the expression my face he realized I was about to explode. He beckoned Bobby and me to follow him into the bedroom, which was equally crowded." Finding no privacy, Jack said to Bobby, "I better talk to Kenny alone in the bathroom." Kenny followed Jack into the "usual Kennedy place," which was the bathroom—the only place they could find real privacy.

Jack leaned against the sink, giving Kenny a minute to contain himself, but it was to no avail. Kenny's voice was low and cold.

"This is the worst mistake you have ever made," Kenny growled. "You came out here to Los Angeles like a knight on a white charger, the clean-cut Ivy League college guy who's promising to get rid of the old hack politicians. And now, in your first move after you get the nomination, you go against all the people who supported you. Are we going to spend the campaign apologizing for Lyndon Johnson and trying to explain why he voted against everything you ever stood for?"

Jack pulled himself up straight, wincing in pain as he did so. His face became pale, livid with anger, so upset and hurt that it took him a moment before he was able to collect himself.

"Wait a minute, Kenny," he said. "I've offered it to him, but he hasn't accepted it yet and maybe he won't. If he does accept it, let's get one thing clear—" Later, in November 1963, as Kenny stood outside the new president's cabin on Air Force One, with Jack Kennedy's body lying in the back of the plane with his widow, Kenny remembered what Jack had said that day in Los Angeles: "Let's get one thing clear. I'm forty-three years old and I am the healthiest candidate for President of the United States. You've traveled with me enough to know that. I am not going to die in office. So the vice presidency thing doesn't mean any-thing. I've been thinking of something else, the leadership of Senate. If we win, we will win by a slim margin and I won't be able to live with Lyndon Johnson as the leader of a small major-ity in the Senate. Did it occur to you that if Lyndon becomes the vice president, I'll have Mike Mansfield as the leader of the Senate, somebody I can trust and depend on?"

Kenny admitted later that as he listened to Jack explain his reasoning, his own views began to soften—not change, but soften a bit.

"If Johnson and Rayburn leave here mad at me," Jack con-tinued, leaning back again against the sink, "they'll ruin me in Congress next month. Then I'll be the laughingstock of the country. Nixon will say I haven't any power in my own party, and I'll lose the election before Labor Day. So I've got to make peace now with Johnson and Rayburn, and offering Lyndon the vice presidency, whether he accepts it or not, is one way of keeping him friendly until Congress adjourns. Explain that to your labor leaders and their liberal friends. All of this is more important to calm southern votes, which I won't get anyway with the Catholic thing working against me. I doubt if Lyndon will even be able to carry Texas, as Dave Lawrence and all the other pols out in the other room claim he will."

With that Jack opened the door and told Bobby to join. "Now listen, Bobby," Jack said, "the two of you go and see Walter Reuther and George Meaney and get to work on them. But don't tell them anything I've said to you about offering Lyndon the vice presidency, so we can have Mike Mansfield as the leader in the Senate. Lyndon won't like that either."

The next issue was explaining the decision to labor and civil rights leaders. The meeting went far worse than either Bobby or Kenny had anticipated. "They savaged Bobby," Kenny said later. "Really just verbally tore him to shreds." Kenny didn't fare much better, nearly coming to blows with several of the labor folks before Bobby intervened and cooler heads prevailed.

"When we left there it was our belief that they planned a floor fight if we put up Johnson for the nomination and such a messy scene would certainly doom Jack Kennedy's candidacy," Kenny said. As they walked back from the hotel and returned to the Biltmore to tell Jack, Kenny had never seen Bobby so shaken. "If they fight the nomination," Bobby said to Kenny, stopping at one point to pull himself together, "even if we beat it back and keep Johnson, Jack is going to leave here a damaged candidate." Kenny completely agreed and said, "All we can hope is that Lyndon said no."

By the time they returned to Jack's crowded suite, his expression told them otherwise. Lyndon, at the urging of Sam Rayburn and others, had said yes.

Bobby and Kenny followed Jack back into the bathroom, which was now converted to a sort of private office, and told Jack the bad news about the meeting with labor. "If we put up Lyndon, they plan to fight the nomination with a floor fight and a candidate of their own," Bobby explained.

The three men stood shoulder to shoulder in the tiny space. Jack sighed. "A fight like that will tear the place apart," Kenny said. He was stating the obvious, of course. The brothers gave Kenny a *thanks, tell us something we don't know* stare.

Jack shook his head. "Well, it is too late now. Lyndon has said yes and we cannot withdraw it. Bobby, you go talk to him. Explain what happened with labor and if he still wants it knowing there might be a floor fight, then it is his."

Bobby nodded. His face still ashen from the verbal beating he had just endured. "We can only hope he changes his mind," Kenny said. Bobby splashed some water on his face and went to the phone to call Johnson's suite and then headed down there to explain the situation they now faced.

"Frankly," Kenny said later, "as I recall it, Bobby said nothing one way or the other. He simply went down to do what Jack had asked him to do. I was the one who objected the most. What happened between Bobby and Lyndon still puzzles me, but now understanding how insecure Lyndon was around Bobby and knowing how direct and undiplomatic Bobby can be sometimes, it is no wonder that they both, in my view, misread each other and the situation."

In truth, nobody knows exactly what happened next, but many legends and stories have cropped up. Whatever happened, it permanently changed the relationship between Bobby and

Lyndon. And the change would have profound effects that not even Kenny could escape in the wake of Jack's murder.

What we do know has been pieced together by conversations Kenny had with Bobby and, later, with Lyndon Johnson and Sam Rayburn. "The entire truth," Kenny said, "probably falls somewhere in between the various versions." Bobby went down to see Lyndon in his suite. When he got there, Bobby found Johnson along with Rayburn and John Connally. Bobby told Kenny later that his stomach immediately tightened.

As he told Kenny, Bobby "went to explain to them that Lyndon might want to withdraw if there was a floor fight with labor and the civil rights groups."

Johnson sat in stunned silence for a moment, then Bobby shocked them further by turning to Sam Rayburn and asking if Lyndon would want to give up the job as majority leader, "to become, say, chairman of the Democratic National Committee?" Rayburn was incredulous. Connally was stunned. And Johnson was speechless, telling Kenny years later that all he could recall at that moment was the day he told Bobby off at the Senate. He wondered if this "some kind of payback? An attempt to publicly embarrass me?"

"Shit!" Rayburn said before he rose and he and Johnson stormed into the other room to consider Bobby's words.

Kenny later said that "Bobby's errand was completely misinterpreted by Sam Rayburn first and then by Johnson, who assumed Bobby was asking Lyndon to withdraw."

Kenny insisted this was not Bobby's intention, but still the damage had been done.

While Bobby waited impatiently in the other room, Rayburn and Johnson panicked in the bedroom. A call was quickly put in to Jack's suite upstairs. Jack was startled as he listened to Lyndon and Sam talk. How the hell could such a simple errand go wrong?

Thinking on his feet, with no time to tell Kenny to call Bobby, Jack employed a tactic they had used quite effectively in the 1952 campaign.

Jack said clearly, "Oh, Bobby has been out of touch and doesn't know what's happening."

Later, Dave Powers remembered it differently. According to Dave, Jack told Rayburn, "I've announced that Lyndon will be the vice-presidential candidate, and Dave Lawrence has agreed to nominate him, Sam. Can you put Lyndon on the telephone?"

Jack then assured a shaken Lyndon that if he was willing to engage in a floor fight with the labor leaders, the nomination was his. Johnson assured Jack he still wanted the job and would take on such a floor fight.

Jack then asked Lyndon to put Bobby on the telephone. Bobby was called into the bedroom to take the call. He told Kenny later that as he walked in and took the telephone from Lyndon, both Sam and Lyndon gave him "these ice-cold stares, and I had no idea what the problem was until I heard Jack's voice."

Bobby got on the telephone and Jack said, "Forget the errand, it's done. Come back up here."

After Bobby hung up the telephone in Johnson's suite, he and Johnson stood face to face. Johnson said, "If the candidate will have me, I will join him in making the fight." Bobby later told Kenny, "I wanted to say, why the hell didn't you just say that in the first place?"

Bobby lamented to Kenny that he was "exhausted and frustrated" by the entire mix-up and felt as though he was banging his head against a wall. "This is going to come back on me," he added. "I just know it."

At the time, Kenny shook his head, "Nobody will remember this, Bobby. Don't worry about it." But later he admitted that "Lyndon never forgot it and every time the story got retold, it sounded worse."

It would be reported by those who were less than kind on the Kennedy side that "Lyndon stood with his lower lip trembling and was near tears."

Kenny was clear: "Bobby never said anything like that. He never said any such thing. Those were stories designed to make Lyndon look bad, which came back to haunt Bobby in the wake of the president's murder. But Bobby never said any such thing. The truth was that Bobby was just sorry he'd gotten into the whole episode. He never said anything to mock or disrespect Lyndon and would not have done. By this point Bobby was just exhausted and wanted the entire episode over with."

Ironically, after all that the drama unfolding over Johnson's selection never did unfold. Around 7:30 p.m., Jack Conway, UAW president Walter Reuther's top aide and Kenny's pal, called Kenny.

"Stop worrying," Conway told Kenny. "There will be no floor fight and no candidate would be put up in opposition to Johnson." Kenny found out later that Reuther had worked out a peace pact of sorts with Johnson to avoid the floor fight. Johnson, ever the savvy political operator, had gone to work on Reuther as soon as Bobby had left his suite. Reuther laid out his terms and Lyndon quickly agreed to everything, which was easy enough. He even agreed to put in writing his support for the party's civil rights platform. In truth Johnson had already twice introduced modest, nevertheless at the time ground-breaking, civil rights legislation in Congress. While both bills had failed in the southern-controlled Senate, his previous attempts made it easier to agree to Reuther's terms than either Reuther or the Kennedy brothers, for that matter, may have realized at the time.

On Friday, July 15, John F. Kennedy's acceptance speech would, for the first time, use a phrase that would come to symbolize his one thousand days of office. Kenny and Bobby remembered it well. In Kenny's words, "he was tired after the grind of the convention, and the sun was shining in his eyes—but it was a speech all of us remembered because it was his first mention of the 'New Frontier.'" Kenny called Helen at home in Washington that night. "This was what we had worked for and believed in," he told his wife. "This was our generation's moment."

Recalling the speech, Johnson said, "I loved that phrase and remember thinking if we could win, it would be a new chapter for our party and this country. We had so much hope."

CHAPTER FOUR
THE EXERCISE OF POWER

President Kennedy did everything possible to make Lyndon feel comfortable, but with little success. "As vice president, Johnson did a slow burn for three years watching the constant buildup of Bobby Kennedy in the press and on television by Bobby's aides in the Justice Department and by many of his friends in the press corps," Kenny said. "The truth was the buildup was tremendous and even President Kennedy made note of it a few times, but always with amusement." But Johnson did not find any of it amusing.

"In fact," Kenny went on, "Bobby himself was not too conscious of the buildup that he was getting, and he was entirely unconscious and completely unaware of the irritation that it was getting to Johnson." Johnson was not well suited to the number two spot in the white house. Despite the best intentions of Jack Kennedy and others early on, Johnson hated being a man without power. Kenny continued:

As vice president, he felt sidelined and ignored, and sorely missed the patronage and power in Texas he had enjoyed when

he was majority leader in the Senate. Johnson blamed everyone else for his unhappiness and placed most of the blame
on Bobby Kennedy. He truly believed that Bobby had taken
over his rightful position as the number two man in government, and that was true enough. Hell, even the president
mentioned Bobby's rising profile. The president mentioned
with some amusement that many of Bobby's friends in the
administration, who were always trying to push Bobby
into running the State Department as well as the Justice
Department, looked upon the younger brother as the real
number one man in government.

Of course it was easier for the president to laugh it off. It was
not so easily overlooked by Johnson, who found himself either
not included or simply uninvited to important meetings run
by Bobby and his friends in the government. While Kenny
knew Bobby was far too busy to engineer such slights, all of
this began to build up. As Kenny put it:

> There was a sense of real resentment in Lyndon and not
> entirely without justification. The president perhaps under-
> stood Lyndon's resentment of Bobby's rising star, more than
> Lyndon may have realized at the time. I remember well how
> annoyed President Kennedy was one day when he went to a
> meeting in the White House with Bobby and several of his
> assistants from the Justice Department and found televi-
> sion cameras and sound-recording equipment in the room.
> It was to be a rather sensitive and confidential discussion on
> the timing of the administration's civil rights bill. The pres-
> ident and the vice president, Larry O'Brien, our congressio-
> nal liaison, and myself felt the new civil rights bill should
> follow the new tax reduction bill for political reasons.
>
> But Bobby and the Justice Department wanted to be

lead on the legislation and push the bill forward themselves. This was all to be documented for this documentary which was supposed to show Bobby and the Justice Department pushing ahead on civil rights with the president and vice president on camera asking them to stall for a while.

Needless to say, the president and especially the vice president were none too happy about being asked to be background players in a television documentary that showed Bobby championing civil rights. To put it mildly, the president did not feel comfortable sparring with Bobby and his Justice Department aides over civil rights before a television camera. I don't think at that moment Bobby realized that his press people had put the president, and vice president for that matter, in an embarrassing position.

Kenny insisted that "Bobby, whose reputed ruthless heart was actually as soft as a marshmallow, never wanted to cause anybody any embarrassment, least of all his brother, the president. The president, the much tougher of the Kennedy brothers, was furious and called me into his office afterward and, in front of the vice president, said if that were ever to happen again, Pierre Salinger, our press secretary would have his head handed to him and be out of a job."

The president further insisted Kenny take a look at the tape before it aired. Kenny did so. The president asked him, "How did I look?" Kenny shrugged and had to admit, "You looked like a frightened antelope and Lyndon didn't look much better."

"Kill the damn tape," the president said, "and go see your pal Bobby and make sure this doesn't happen again."

"How come he is my pal when he screws up?" Kenny asked, trying to lighten the mood.

The president was not amused. Arrangements were made

with the network to kill the tape. Kenny called Bobby to have lunch at the Pink Elephant, a sandwich place near the Justice Department, and let Bobby know just how upset the president had been by the entire incident.

"Bobby was shocked. He was so focused on doing the right thing, especially when it came to civil rights. He admitted he simply had not thought it through."

Kenny left to return to the White House, satisfied that he had done his job and the incident was over. Which was why, a few days later, Kenny, who had thought the issue addressed, was surprised when he was called into the Oval Office, where the president sat in his rocking chair with a clearly seething Lyndon Johnson just behind him. The entire event had sort of been eating at Johnson since it had happened.

"Kenny," Jack said sternly, "please explain to the vice president what you did about the tape from the documentary?"

Kenny, in a system that he and the president had worked out in advance and used many times since 1952, pretended to look chagrined.

He then explained that he "had made arrangements to have the tape killed by the network." Further, he had met with Bobby and had made clear to Bobby that "this was unacceptable and could not happen again."

Lyndon seemed somewhat pacified and said that while he hated to gang up on Bobby, "you cannot run a government and make decisions by television camera."

Kenny agreed. He explained that Bobby felt badly and in the end the vice president went away feeling somewhat better:

The point was that while the president was really upset with Bobby over the incident, we dealt with it and it was over, but Lyndon always saw all these motives behind every move Bobby made. He firmly came to believe, for example, that the entire incident had been engineered to embarrass the vice president and draw him out. In order to have him make some mistake on civil rights that would then humiliate him in public. The truth was Bobby just never thought it through, not from the president's perspective or the vice president's. I am not even sure Bobby knew the vice president was going to be in the meeting.

The end result of these types of situations was to make the vice president overly cautious, pull back, and at a certain point he rarely if ever spoke at meetings. He would explain to Kenny that he preferred to do his "talking in private, directly to the president."

"Even when the president would try to draw him out, it was often to no avail. He was just convinced that Bobby and other 'Kennedy men,' as he called them, looked down at him and were determined to embarrass him in front of Jack Kennedy and the public," Kenny said. "He withdrew even further, which made him even less effective and proved frustrating as hell to the president, who was not a man who understood nor tolerated such insecurity."

The more Lyndon withdrew, the more the president became frustrated and the more it damaged their relationship. But nothing Kenny said to Lyndon could get him to budge. "In the end, I think he came to trust me the most in those days. He knew I was a straight shooter, never played games, and always told him the truth. I also always made sure his calls got answered immediately and his access to the president was unfettered."

Lyndon was appreciative of Kenny's honesty and came to trust his judgment, especially when it came to dealing with the president or Bobby.

One evening when waiting to see President Kennedy in the

Oval Office, Kenny got himself and Johnson a drink. Lyndon took a few sips and then said what was on his mind. Seated on the edge of Kenny's desk, which was just outside the Oval Office with easy access to the president, Johnson leaned forward into Kenny's physical space, a Lyndon trademark and an effective habit that Kenny and the Kennedy brothers hated. But Lyndon had something he wanted Kenny to understand.

Lyndon told Kenny plainly: "Look, I know Bobby is your friend, but he doesn't like me. No matter what, he doesn't like anything I do or say. The one thing I know is that you always treat me fairly and never lie or mislead me. You are one of the few fellas in this place I can trust. I appreciate that."

"President Kennedy was always uncomfortably aware of Johnson's unhappiness in the vice presidency and leaned over backwards in an effort to keep him involved in important government affairs and to give him a feeling of participation in the important affairs of the administration," Kenny said.

In fact, Kenny reported that President Kennedy had issued a firm order that everybody in the White House was to be courteous and considerate with Johnson and he put Kenny in charge of seeing that the order was not ignored.

"I became friendly with LBJ and his aides," Kenny recalled. "I became very friendly with Walter Jenkins and Bill Moyers and spent evenings with Lyndon having a few drinks and listening to his problems and complaints, which in my view were mostly imaginary because he wasn't being slighted in the way he claimed. This continued throughout my year with him after President Kennedy had been murdered. It became sort of custom. He would talk and I would listen. He knew both during his time as vice president and as president that anything he said would go no further [than me]."

According to Kenny, "The president always included him in the National Security Council meetings and Congressional leadership meetings and tried without much success to get him to participate in the policy discussions. Johnson was given the responsibility for directing the space program and was sent on important overseas missions. The president loved it when Johnson invited a camel driver from Pakistan to come to Washington."

"If I tried that," Kennedy said, "I would have ended up with camel dung all over the White House lawn."

Kennedy wanted Johnson to feel he had access equal to that of Bobby. Kenny said, "Only two men in government were given the special privilege of entering the president's office at any time unseen through the back door from the garden, without following the normal procedure from the front door through my office. Neither of them ever abused the privilege and seldom came to see the president without calling me first. Johnson called and asked to see the president often with personal complaints, frequently about Bobby."

Kenny and the president developed a strategy to deal with such circumstances:

> The president would first hear him out alone, and then call me into his office and denounce me in front of Johnson for whatever the vice president was beefing about. I would humbly take the blame and promise to correct the situation, and the vice president would go away somewhat happier.
>
> I remember one day when another one of Johnson's complaints to President Kennedy once again involved Bobby ("That kid brother of yours") as well as Sarah T. Hughes, the same lifelong Texas friend who later . . . would be asked to swear Johnson in as president in the hot and sticky cabin of Air Force One after the assassination. Hughes was up for consideration for a federal judgeship in Texas.
>
> "Damn it, Kenny, you've gone and done it again,"

the president said when he called Kenny into the office. "Lyndon, you go ahead and tell him yourself what happened this time."

Johnson began this long tale of woe as he usually did, quoting John Nance Garner describing the vice presidency as a thankless office with as much prestige as a pitcher of warm spit, but Johnson used another word in the place of spit.

He went on to explain he had requested that his friend Sarah Hughes be appointed to a federal judgeship in Texas. He owed her much and it was the least he could do. The Justice Department's "friends of your kid brother Bobby" got back to him and explained that Sarah was sixty-five and therefore too old to be considered for a federal judgeship. Johnson then offered the name of another Dallas lawyer and then called Sarah to explain the situation. He said she took the news very graciously.

The vice president was then sent to Berlin along with Secretary of State Dean Rusk to show the American flag and reassure Berliners of our commitment. When he returned he learned to his embarrassment that Sarah Hughes had indeed been given the federal judgeship after all.

As it turned out, while Johnson was out of the country Bobby had been on Capitol Hill and ran into Speaker Sam Rayburn. Bobby pressured Rayburn about a few bills the Justice Department was eager to get out of the Judiciary Committee. Rayburn suggested to Bobby that his bills "might never get out of committee if my good friend Sarah Hughes doesn't get her appointment." Bobby, frustrated, quickly explained that Sarah Hughes was too old and all this had been explained to Vice President Johnson.

The wily old Rayburn smiled and shook his head, "Son, everybody looks old to you. Do you want those bills passed or don't you?"

The next day Sarah T. Hughes was appointed and Bobby's bills were passed out of committee.

Johnson stamped his foot in the Oval Office and cried out, "Mr. President, you realize where this leaves me? Sarah Hughes now thinks I am a nothing. The lawyer I offered the job to after your kid brother turned Sarah down, thinks I am the biggest liar and fool in the history of the state of Texas. All on account of that kid brother of yours!"

We sat in silence for a moment, and then the president couldn't help from laughing and I did as well. At that point even Johnson saw the humor. In the end, a few calls were made to Hughes and the other lawyer to straighten out the situation.

As for Bobby, he just shrugged it off when he Kenny told him about the situation: "I am too busy to worry about that kind of stuff."

Both President Kennedy and Kenny, at the president's direction, bent over backwards to accommodate Johnson's insecurity, but with limited success. According to Kenny, "President Kennedy was uncomfortably aware of Johnson's unhappiness in the vice presidency. Each incident real or imagined seemed to make the situation worse. And as Bobby's profile began to rise, pushed in the press by many of Bobby's loyal aides at Justice, columnists began to speculate about Bobby replacing Johnson in the number two slot in 1964." Still, despite the rumors around Washington, Kenny was clear that John Kennedy had no intention of dumping Johnson in 1964.

"At first the president dismissed the talk. It was so foolish, neither he, nor Bobby for that matter, would consider such a move." But the talk began to gain steam, aided as it was by the real rumors of Johnson's unhappiness as vice president. All this was swirling around Washington in November 1963.

As Kenny worked with Johnson's staff to plan the Texas trip, Kennedy saw it as the first step in his 1964 campaign.

As he swam in the White House pool, the president asked Dave Powers to get him the figures for Texas. The next morning Dave had the latest figures at the ready. "The president was a great man for small details, always the perfectionist," Dave said. "When I showed him the figures that morning, he was delighted." He returned to the Oval Office and called Kenny in to share them with him.

"Texas and Florida, Kenny, I am telling you, those are the two key states for the 1964 campaign," the president said. The weekend before the Texas trip the president had been in Florida campaigning. Texas was the next logical stop.

"When he saw those figures," Kenny insisted, "nobody had to force President Kennedy to go to Texas, least of all Lyndon Johnson. He could not have been held back from going there. He was looking forward to it, especially once Jackie had agreed to join him."

Still, as the planning proceeded for the Texas trip, Johnson remained reluctant. Kenny explained:

> Johnson had not been closely involved in the planning of the upcoming campaign and had begun to suspect that Bobby Kennedy and his allies were planning to dump him as the vice-presidential candidate in 1964 because of his connection with Bobby Baker, the Johnson protégé whose scandals case had just been revealed. Johnson was convinced that Bobby Kennedy had been behind the exposure of Baker, a ridiculous assumption because a scandal of any kind in Washington reflecting on the Democrats was the last thing the Kennedys wanted. Bobby would never have wanted anything that might hurt his brother's reelection effort.

According to Bobby, the president "never had any intention of dumping Johnson." It was a position Kenny concurred with completely:

> I was sitting with the president and George Smathers on the way to Florida the Saturday before the Texas trip. Senator Smathers asked him if he was planning to get rid of Johnson because of the Baker case. Smathers said rumors were flying all over the Capitol that he planned to dump Johnson in favor of Bobby. "If I've heard them then he has," Smathers said.
>
> The president glanced at Smathers and said, "George, you must be the dumbest man in the world. If I drop Lyndon, it will make it look as if we have a really bad and serious scandal on our hands in the Bobby Baker case, which we haven't, and that will reflect on me. It will look as though I made a mistake in picking Johnson in 1960, and can you imagine the mess of trying to select somebody to replace him? Bobby is my brother and he cares deeply that we succeed in 1964, do you seriously believe he would do anything to jeopardize that success? The dumbest thing we could do is dump Johnson. And, George, I am not dumb."
>
> For Jack Kennedy that was the end of the discussion. He said to me as we left for Texas, "Johnson stays on the ticket. We cannot win without him."

But Johnson was not anxious for the president to go to Texas, Kenny later recalled,

> which is contrary to many stories that appeared after the president was murdered. He did not want the president to see for himself how little prestige and influence the vice president had in his own home state. Since he had joined

the New Frontier ticket, his fellow conservatives in Texas had largely turned against him. The more liberal Texas Democrats, such as Senator Ralph Yarborough, had always been against him because he was looked upon as a conservative. Vice President Johnson felt sidetracked and ignored. He told many that he sorely missed the patronage and power he had enjoyed back in Texas when he was majority leader in the Senate.

Without that power and the ability to wield such influence, Johnson felt that he no longer was a player in Texas politics. He was against the Texas trip mostly because he feared that his lack of influence and popularity would become obvious to president and then that Bobby might use that evidence along with the growing Bobby Baker scandal to dump him from the ticket. Kenny recalled:

When I discussed this months later—after Dallas—with Bobby, he was dumbfounded. He said, "That decision, the vice-presidential spot, had been Jack's alone in 1960 and would be the same in 1964. My last conversation with [Jack] about this issue, which had been during the summer, he made clear that he was very pleased with Johnson and felt he was necessary for us to win in 1964." Bobby shook his head in disgust and said "Kenny, where does he get all this stuff?" I shook my head. I really couldn't say, but as I've said right along, it was mostly imagined by Johnson. "When I spoke to him about the trip to Texas," Bobby said, "he was looking forward to raising some serious money for the Democratic National Committee coffers, and to just jumping into the political waters again. He said to me that he loved campaigning and really saw this as the start of 1964. He told me he couldn't wait to go. That Jackie was joining him made it all the more fun from his perspective. It was only later I read all these accounts about his not wanting to go to Texas and his being upset with Johnson. That was all news to me and I will say all those accounts were from people who were not there."

In November 1963 with an eye towards the '64 campaign, President Kennedy was going to Texas to raise money and refill the depleted Democratic National Committee coffers in preparation for the national campaign. Kenny recalled: "He had been pressing a reluctant Governor John Connally to stage a fund-raising event for the party, and Connally, who had no desire to be marked as a Kennedy supporter in Texas, had been stalling him off." In October 1963, Connally finally arrived at the White House to meet with Kenny and the president about a potential Texas fund-raiser. "It was to be a big $100-a-plate dinner in Austin following a midday visit to Dallas. Johnson was furious because Connally had not bothered to invite him to the White House for that meeting with the president. I had not included Johnson, because I mistakenly assumed he and Connally had already discussed the trip."

The president had also timed the trip so that he could appear at a testimonial dinner for representative Albert Thomas from Houston, the congressman's hometown. Kenny explained:

The elderly Thomas was one of the president's favorite congressmen and had done an important fiscal favor for Kennedy in his capacity as chairman of the subcommittee that approved supplementary appropriations. Thomas had been key in helping to raise the money necessary for the launching of the president's beloved space program. The president felt deeply indebted to Thomas, who had helped put the money together for the program. He also understood that NASA had picked Houston over Boston or somewhere in the Midwest for one reason—Albert Thomas.

Kenny remembered that the president had spoken privately to Thomas, who it was rumored would soon retire, about staying on. Later, in the wake of Kennedy's death, Thomas told Kenny of their last fateful conversation in Texas: "Listen Albert, I'd like you to stay on—as long as I do. I don't know how long that will be."

But while much has been made of Kennedy's trip as an attempt to patch up the political feud between Governor Connally and Senator Ralph Yarborough, a feud that Johnson had been incapable of solving, the truth was the trip to Texas was "to get the 1964 campaign off to a strong early start."

"The coming election year looked good," Kenny said.

The economy was booming and the Saturn I rocket, which the president had just inspected at Cape Canaveral a few days earlier, was to be launched in December. But still, he cautioned us there was "a lot of hard work ahead." He believed that, as he put it to me one evening just before we left for Texas, "the prejudice against [his] Catholicism . . . the canonical impediment," was as dead an issue as many Americans, including his own staff, assumed it to be. "This time they will use my stance against civil rights as an excuse." We discussed our plan, which was to campaign hard in Texas and in Florida because he knew he had little hope of winning any other southern states.

Later, after the president's death, when Kenny was over at the DNC as executive director in a bid to ensure Lyndon Johnson's reelection and thus carry on John Kennedy's legacy, he would recall that night's conversation with President Kennedy:

> The president told me that "Barry Goldwater would go on to win Alabama, Georgia, Louisiana, Mississippi, and South Carolina." And while the president would have found it difficult to believe that the Republicans would select Barry Goldwater, the right-wing senator from Arizona, his prediction of how the states would go turned out to be dead on. His firm belief that the states would go that way made the trip to Texas all the more important. Contrary to reports he either dreaded or was annoyed by having to take the trip, he told me saw it as the kickoff to the campaign and couldn't wait to get started.

CHAPTER FIVE
DALLAS, TEXAS, NOVEMBER 22, 1963

The motorcade in Dallas was about to turn onto Dealey Plaza. All of Kenny's fears and uneasiness about the Texas trip had been erased. Texas seemed to be simply wild about John and Jackie Kennedy. As the motorcade carrying President John F. Kennedy took a sharp right into Dealey Plaza in downtown Dallas, Dave looked down at his watch. "It is just 12:30 p.m.," he said. "We are due at the Trade Mart luncheon now."

"It's fine," Kenny said, "we are only five minutes from there now, so we are only running five minutes behind schedule."

Kenny had just finished speaking when they heard three cracks—two shots close together, then a third. The sound ricocheted across Dealey Plaza. The cracks were loud enough to be heard over the roar of the screaming, enthusiastic crowds lining the streets. The sounds could have been a car backfiring, but the sick feeling in Kenny's stomach told him this was something entirely different.

"I remember it all began so beautifully," Lady Bird Johnson said.

After a drizzle in the morning, the sun came out bright and beautiful. We were going into Dallas. In the lead car, President and Mrs. Kennedy, John and Nellie Connally, and then a Secret Service car full of men, and then our car—Lyndon and me and Senator Yarborough. The streets were lined with people, lots and lots of people, the children all smiling, placards, confetti, people waving from windows. Our last happy moment . . . was looking up and seeing Mary Griffith leaning out of a window waving at me. Mary for many years had been in charge of altering the clothes which I purchased at a Dallas store. Then, almost at the edge of town, on our way to the Trade Mart where we were going to have luncheon, we were rounding a curve, going down a hill, and suddenly there was a sharp, loud report—a shot. It seemed to me it came from a building from my right above my shoulder. Then a moment and then two more shots in rapid succession. There was such a gala air, I thought it must be firecrackers or some sort of celebration. Then the Secret Service men were suddenly down in the lead car. I heard over the radio system, "Let's get out of here!"

"What was that? Was that firecrackers?" Dave asked Kenny as they rode in the backup car directly behind the president's limousine. They had just turned into Dealey Plaza and were just across from the Texas School Book Depository.

It had been gunfire. Dave knew it as well as Kenny. Dave said later, "I just did not want to say it out loud."

"The next bullet," Kenny would later recall, "took off part of the president's head, sending blood and brains everywhere, then lifting him like a rag doll out of his seat and dropping him out of sight."

"He's dead," was Kenny's only comment, not meaning to even say it out loud.

Dave looked over at him in horror.

As the motorcade sped up, racing to Parkland Hospital, Kenny already knew—though he prayed he was wrong. His gut told him something else. Having been shot down a few times behind enemy lines and still enduring the pain of shrapnel in his right leg, a wound he had received in World War II, in his gut he had that sickening feeling that his beloved president, his friend, was dead.

Then, as the cars started to speed up, he watched helplessly and in horror as Jackie inexplicably climbed out on the back of the car, an act she would later confess she could neither explain nor recall. But for the heroics of Secret Service agent Clint Hill, Kenny and Dave would have been bringing two bodies back, not just one.

"We raced to Parkland Hospital," Lady Bird said. "As we ground to a halt—we were still in the third car—Secret Service men began to pull, lead, guide, and hustle us out. I cast one last look over my shoulder and saw in the president's car a bundle of pink, just like drift blossoms, lying on the back seat. I realized later it was actually Mrs. Kennedy lying over the president's body. They led us to the hospital—a very small room. It was lined with white sheets."

Arriving at Parkland just behind Jack's car, Kenny leaped out before his vehicle had even stopped. He raced to the presidential limousine just in time to see Jackie clutching her husband's body, lying over his body, grasping his shattered head in her lap, cradling him and refusing to let go. His blood and brains were splattered all over her pink suit, face, and hair. As she held his shattered head, Jack's blood began to flood the back seat of the limousine and drip onto the pavement.

Kenny turned away from the sight of Jack's body. For a moment he felt sick and needed to gather himself to be the governmental aide, the president's right hand man in charge of the president's schedule and travel arrangements. Kenny knew it was now up to him to take charge. For the moment, anyway, he needed to put aside his personal feelings and do what had to be done.

As the doctors arrived with the gurney, they pleaded with Jackie to release her steely grip on her husband's body. Jackie, without speaking, flatly refused. Secret Service agents Clint Hill and Roy Kellerman had rushed to Jackie's side, and again, it was Clint who seemed, without words, to understand Jackie's concerns. With the press arriving, Jackie was fearful someone would get a photograph of her husband's bloody, shattered head. Hill took off his jacket and together they gently wrapped and covered Jack's head. He was then lifted onto the gurney and they all began to race towards the trauma room at Parkland.

Jackie, running alongside the gurney in her bloodstained suit, was still clutching the coat around Jack's head. At one point it began to slip and Jackie made her first sound. It was a quick outward gasp as she quickly replaced the coat.

As they reached the trauma room, the doctors raced Jack inside, refusing to allow Jackie to join them. A nurse found a folding chair for Jackie to sit on outside the trauma room. Jackie had heard one of the doctors say that Jack still had a faint pulse; apparently his heart was still pumping and his lungs were still breathing.

"Kenny," Jackie said softly as he paced back and forth in front of her, "do you think . . ." She never completed the thought.

Kenny was relieved, and he did not answer her. He had seen the vacant stare in Jack's eyes out in the car, all the blood, and seen how limp his body had been when moved to the gurney. Kenny knew, given that last shot, that Jack was dead. But he said none of this to Jackie.

When Dave arrived, Kenny excused himself to go find Lyndon Johnson. At this stage, Kenny had to begin to focus on the next steps. It kept his mind from focusing on the horror he had just witnessed. It was now time to tell Lyndon Johnson the horrendous news.

Lady Bird, who was sitting with Lyndon just down the hall, recalled:

> Through it all Lyndon was remarkably calm and quiet. He said we had better move the plane to another part of the field. He spoke of going back out to the plane in black cars. Every face that came in, you searched for answers. I think the face I kept seeing it on was Kenny O'Donnell, who loved him so much. When he came in, we knew immediately from his face and his voice that the president was dead. Everything had changed. It was from Kenny O'Donnell Lyndon and I heard the words, "The president is dead."

The next step was to get Lyndon Johnson, now the president of the United States, to safety. Kenny told Johnson point blank that they did not know what the hell was going on, given the situation and recent political events. "It might be a conspiracy," he admitted.

Johnson nodded numbly. "I am in your hands, Kenny," he said solemnly.

Kenny later explained, "What happened next, well, it was a misunderstanding, which, given the terrible circumstances, is understandable. Of course, President Johnson then compounded this with his stories, which were inaccurate, but . . . everything is a conspiracy to him . . . Lyndon and I had the discussion that it might be a conspiracy. You know the president had just been murdered. I felt and he agreed that it might be a conspiracy and that now President Johnson should leave.

This was a very proper judgment to make at that time. He agreed. I had already sent agents to cover Speaker of the House John McCormack.

"Remember," Kenny noted sadly, "the Secret Service is my responsibility. My job and their job is to cover and protect the president. Today, we had failed. I did not want something to happen to Lyndon. This reality weighed on me heavily."

The decision for Johnson to leave Parkland Hospital and go directly to Air Force One at Love Field was one Kenny and Lyndon made together. Johnson would then proceed to Washington. Kenny would stay with Jackie in Dallas and then follow the new president back to Washington and they would bring Jack's body back.

As far as Kenny was concerned, his job remained to take care of Jackie and the dead president. Once Johnson was gone, Kenny figured Johnson would be in good hands. It never occurred to Kenny that he would have been expected to play a role for the new president.

"Lyndon and I were in agreement on this," Kenny recalled. "We don't know what has happened or what is going on. John Kennedy has just been murdered in front of us. We are all in a daze anyway. We discussed whether he should go back to Bergstrom Air Force Base where he would get some police security, military police."

Kenny shook his head, "No," he said to Johnson. He then urged Johnson to instead go directly to Love Field and take Air Force One back to Washington. "If it was a conspiracy, nobody would know what hospital we are at, where he was coming from or going. The newspapers would not have time to report it and speed, we felt, was a necessity. The key was to get him back to Washington, which he agreed to do. He was terrific. He said, 'I am in your hands. Anything you want me to do, Kenny, I will do.'"

Johnson then told his staff, "Kenny O'Donnell is in charge of everything."

"[Johnson] was positively terrific. Look, Johnson was in a state of shock himself. He is now President of the United States. He suddenly has all this on his shoulders and he was in a bit of shock. Understandable. We all were. Anyone who says they were not and were there at that time is a liar. Everybody was numb. Disbelief. We were in disbelief. I walked him to the car," Kenny recalled.

As Kenny stood there holding the car door, Johnson said, as Kenny remembered it, "he would head to Love Field and meet me at the White House in Washington. We did not know at this time what was going on and my job was to get the fallen president and his widow home safely. Once Johnson was safely off, I could focus on that job and he got in the car and that was the last I saw of him. He drove off and, I felt, into history."

Kenny also recalled, "My job has ended, as I saw it. My job is now to serve my president and his widow. Get him home. Johnson is now president and he has other obligations. He has obligations to the country. He cannot be worried about us."

Within minutes of Kennedy being declared dead, Kenny knew Jackie would not leave Dallas without her husband. He explained this to the medical examiner, a man Kenny thought was a "horse's ass," who refused to budge on his position that the president's body could not leave Dallas. According to state law, since this was a murder, the president's body had to remain in Dallas for an autopsy.

The medical examiner, Dr. Earl Rose, told Kenny and Jackie that the president's body now belonged to the state of Texas and, as he put it, "I am in charge. He now belongs to me."

"Like hell he does and like hell you are," Kenny told him point blank. His voice was low and menacing as he moved toward Dr. Rose, who quickly backed up.

"Kenny," Jackie said, her voice bringing him back to his job, which was to get Jack home and to protect his widow.

"Let me be clear. You are in charge of nothing," Kenny snarled at Rose, who no doubt was grateful for Jackie's intervention.

Calls were made, as Kenny recalled, higher authorities were appealed to, but nobody could budge Dr. Rose. As Jackie began to fall apart, Kenny's Irish temper boiled over. This time there was no Jack or Bobby to hold him back.

With Jack's body in a casket on the gurney, Kenny ordered the Dallas police and doctors to move. "Get the hell out of the way. We are leaving," he said.

They refused. Kenny then told them to go to hell and with Dave on one side, Jackie behind him, and the Secret Service at his side, they plowed through the men, sending several to the ground. Placing the body in an ambulance, Jackie and Dave jumped in the back; Kenny opened the driver's door, pulled out the startled driver, took the keys, and they sped off with Secret Service in tow.

As Kenny watched from the rearview mirror, the Dallas police raced to their cars, many with guns drawn. Kenny gunned the ambulance and headed towards Love Field. They would simply have to outrun the police, get on Air Force Two, and take off before they could be stopped.

"We just broke the law, you know," Dave said to Kenny from the back.

"I don't give a damn about them," was Kenny's cold reply. "We need to take Jack home."

CHAPTER SIX
THE LONG JOURNEY HOME

"Kenny," he heard Jackie say. Her voice startled him and brought him back to the present. He turned to see her gesture to the seat next to her. He sat slowly, feeling suddenly exhausted, numb, and still. As he stared at John F. Kennedy's casket, he was still in disbelief. How did they get here? Was he really gone? Dead? Not possible, Kenny thought to himself. It just cannot be. This was, Kenny believed, his fault. His job was to keep the president safe. All he could do now was try his best to get the president's widow and his body safely back to Bobby in Washington.

"Kenny," she repeated. "I'm thirsty."

Kenny nodded. "I think we could all use a drink," he said.

She nodded wordlessly. Reluctantly, he gently withdrew his hand from hers. He rose slowly and looked over to Dave.

"Dave?" he asked.

The normally ebullient Mr. Powers, Jack Kennedy's beloved little Irishman, was quiet, his face drawn, ashen. He stared blankly at the casket holding his beloved president's body. He was still in utter disbelief.

Kenny shrugged and began to move towards the front of the plane. He and President Kennedy had had to borrow Air Force Two a few times, so Kenny knew well where Lyndon kept some booze, which Kenny could reach without having to engage the president's staff or the president. It was nothing personal; he just did not have the stomach for it.

Carefully, he made his way forward, his mind mentally rewinding the day's events. It had begun beautifully in Fort Worth, Texas, before they flew to Dallas for a parade through the downtown area. The crowds were thick, cheering, and happy and the weather had been beautiful. "Kennedy weather," they had called it throughout the 1960 campaign. This was the first political event of 1964: Jack Kennedy, accompanied for the first time in a long time by his exotically beautiful wife, planned to run and win a second term for the presidency. This made the state of Texas critical, so here they were and the day could not have been more inviting.

There had only been one off note so far, which at the time had seemed minor. Jackie had been consistently late for every event, something which drove the president crazy and upset Jackie. That morning in Fort Worth, Jack explained to Kenny that his wife had been close to tears in the morning over some issue to do with her outfit. Jack had covered it nicely with the press and the public with a chuckling Lyndon by his side, joking, "It does not take Lyndon and I as long to get dressed, but then nobody cares what we look like."

Everyone had laughed, but what was going on behind the scenes was a mess. Jackie's longtime maid, Providencia Paredes, had decided to stay home in Washington for an important school event for her son Gustavo, who happened to be a very close to John Kennedy, Jr. Provi had chosen to stay behind in

Washington and not accompany the Kennedys to Texas. She had been with Jack Kennedy since he first came to Washington. When Jack married Jackie, she became a vital player in helping to create and maintain the image of Jackie, as Kenny and Jack liked to call her, as "Madame La Femme." Given the constant press scrutiny Jackie received, that was no small task.

Mary Gallagher had stepped in to travel with Jackie and the president, and while she was perfectly capable, she was no Provi. Provi knew Jackie so well that she would often anticipate a request from Jackie before she herself had fully constructed the thought.

However, Provi was not there on this trip to Texas, and when Jackie cried to Jack about what a mess things were that morning, Jack demanded a promise from her: "Never leave Provi home again. She is our good luck charm."

It was a minor point, a nothing thing in a day that would loom large over all the survivors. Jackie later told Provi the story through tears when she recounted the day. Provi would be forever haunted by the story, unable to retell it without crying herself.

None of that mattered much to Kenny at the time. His political antenna was focused on the short trip to Dallas and his hopes for a good crowd to greet Jack. Indeed, November 22 promised to be another glorious Texas day. Another day of "Kennedy weather," Kenny thought as he trailed behind, watching as Jack Kennedy slowly climbed the stairs to Air Force One for the short trip to Dallas and the motorcade through the downtown.

Just before going inside the plane, Jack suddenly and quite unexpectedly turned to Kenny and flashed that spectacular Kennedy smile. He looked at Kenny, squeezed his shoulder and said, "It is Kennedy weather. It is going to be our day. Great job today, Kenny."

With that, Jack moved to sit with Jackie. Kenny never spoke to his friend again.

"How the hell did we get here?" Kenny wondered as he made his way to the bar and pulled out three glasses. He began to pour and then thought, the hell with it. He swallowed his in one gulp before grabbing the glasses and the bottle and heading back to Jackie, Dave, and the dead president's body.

As he walked, he recalled how the entire trip had begun—tangled up in Texas politics. "The trip to Texas was purely political," Kenny would later explain. "In fact, the idea for the trip to Texas was started by me," he said with a soul-wrenching regret that would never loosen its grip on him. "It was my idea. I was annoyed because we never get any of that wonderful Texas oil money that I used to read about in the newspapers."

Kenny remembered a conversation back at the White House a few short months before with Vice President Johnson. Kenny stood just to the side of President Kennedy's desk in the Oval Office, his usual spot. His arms were folded in characteristic fashion, a tight smile just around the corners of his mouth as he listened to Jack talk with Lyndon about Texas money and politics. Jack leaned back in his chair, flashing that million-dollar smile at Lyndon.

"I am not questioning you," Jack explained, gesturing towards Kenny with a roll of his eyes, as if to say to Lyndon, but you know Kenny. "But Kenny," Jack continued, almost as if Kenny were not present, "keeps pressing me about all that Texas money that we need."

Lyndon stood, hands in his pockets, looking unhappy, his eyes moving from Jack to Kenny. At first, Kenny said little. This little charade was all prearranged. Jack and Kenny had done it many a time. Kenny would play the political "bad guy" to Jack's "good guy."

"That way," Kenny later explained, "if the vice president

got mad or offended, he could get mad at me, not at President Kennedy."

"All I hear about is how rich you people in Texas are," Kenny said to Johnson, only half teasing. "We are running all over the country campaigning and raising money. The Massachusetts people are screaming bloody murder, because we are bleeding them dry. They keep asking about this Texas money, but we have yet to see any of that famous, much talked about Texas money."

Lyndon laughed—sort of, but not really. He liked Kenny. As a matter of fact, Kenny was one of the few Kennedy people Johnson did like. And, more importantly, he trusted him. But he sure as hell got Kenny's message, even if he did not really want to hear it. He realized he had ducked the president and Kenny for as long as he could. This time he was going to have to, as he himself liked to say, "step in it all the way."

The visual image, Kenny joked later to Jack as they headed to another meeting, was a perfect description of the current Texas political situation.

Texas was, as it had been in the 1960 campaign, critical to the success of Kennedy's election. Jack had used Kenny to deliver a message: "Get your house in order in your home state and start bringing in some of that Texas money."

Kenny explained later:

In 1962, we spent an awful lot of money on congressional campaigns. We took every cent we had and financed congressmen and senators' fights. The president had several major legislative priorities from civil rights to the tax bill to voting rights, and we wanted as many of our guys in there as possible. But it was a costly fight. Now we needed Lyndon to help us make up the deficit.

The Democratic National Committee was dead broke, not that you cannot continue to raise money as president. You can, especially as we approached 1964, but I was saying to Lyndon, only half kidding, half not—where is that Texas money? I pointed out to him once again that in Massachusetts they had raised over three million dollars in the last year. They are starting to complain up there that they are getting a little broke and asking where the hell is all this promised Texas cash? I told him point blank, "Look, we need a new source. The Massachusetts people were complaining they were putting up all the money and they got precious little in return." Which of course was true. Therefore, I had said to the vice president, "What about it? We need some of that famous Texas money you keep bragging about." This went on for four months and finally he agreed to go to Texas.

As Kenny understood all too well from the 1960 campaign, Texas politics had always been of the complicated variety. This political season had been no different. Actually, it had been downright ugly from the vice president's point of view. Kenny and the president were not necessarily unsympathetic; they understood Lyndon's dilemma very well. The reality was that the president just did not really care. Nor did Kenny. They were eyeing 1964 and Jack's reelection and Johnson needed to get his political ducks in a row.

"The reason he did not want to go to Texas was apparent," Kenny recalled. "The president and I understood, but only Lyndon could address the issue. The problem was, of course, Texas senator Ralph Yarborough."

Ralph Webster Yarborough was from Chandler, Texas. Having run unsuccessfully for governor numerous times, he had become well known enough across the state to win the

Senate seat in a special election in 1957. He was a liberal who was a political rival to Governor John Connally, and despite similar backgrounds, he was often at odds with Lyndon Johnson.

Connally had his own problems and at the moment had precious little sympathy for Lyndon's problems with Jack. Connally was fighting with both Lyndon Johnson and Senator Yarborough. In Kenny's words, "it all made for a nasty political mess."

A few months before the Dallas trip, Kenny remembered, during a political swing through El Paso, Texas,

> Governor Connally pulls me aside and begins complaining about everyone, especially his favorite target of the moment, which happened to be Lyndon. It was not a pleasant moment. The president, Vice President Johnson, Governor Connally, and I were having a few drinks in the president's hotel room. John Connally signaled to me he wanted to talk alone. We went into the bedroom and he said to me, "Look, Kenny, you have got to take care of us. Lyndon won't lift a finger to help, because they think he is going to be accused of being another Texas crony. We do live in the country as well, you know! We ought to have some rights to get something from Washington. After all, we did help win the damn presidency. If you do not mind much, I am going to call you directly on our problems."
>
> Lyndon Johnson of course was there, as were Homer Thornberry, Congressman Jim Wright, and a couple of other congressmen. Lyndon knew what Connally was doing; he did not care. He just wouldn't do it. John Connally was true to his word. He called me many times about different problems and we ended up becoming pretty good friends. Lyndon was very sensitive, which was somewhat understandable, though frustrating from our point of view.

Lyndon put up with a lot guff from those guys in Texas, both the president and I felt. Far too much guff.

The Texas trip was set up on that basis; it was designed to raise money and soothe the troubled political waters in Texas as we moved towards the '64 campaign. We wanted no distractions or drama from Texas. Both Connally and Lyndon went over the Yarborough problem with me. The problem was more with John Connally and Yarborough than it ever was between Lyndon and Yarborough. Lyndon and Ralph got along fine, but Yarborough and Connally couldn't stand each other. The dislike had been long-standing and was bordering on becoming all-out political warfare. What made the damn thing worse was that Lyndon had no influence with the Texas delegation. None.

Kenny had explained this with some disgust to Jack over drinks one evening at the White House, shortly before the trip, adding that "neither Yarborough nor Connally give a damn about what Lyndon thinks. They just don't give a damn about his opinion or what he wants."

"What do you mean? None?" Jack had demanded.

He simply could not imagine that after all this time Lyndon had not yet mastered his own Texas delegation. He sure as hell had mastered the United States Senate. As reluctant as he had been, Jack understood well the need to get control of one's own delegation, especially if you have larger ambitions. Hell, getting the Massachusetts delegation under control was one of the first things that Kenny and Larry had done for Jack, even before Jack had wanted them to do it. It had turned out to be a critical and essential political move for Jack's future. Therefore, it was with his own experience in mind that Jack was simply incredulous that Lyndon could not tame the political bickering in his own delegation.

"Here I was," Kenny said, "trying to explain to a rather skeptical President Kennedy that this situation is so bad between these men, that we are faced with the problem that Senator Yarborough would not even ride in the car with Johnson. Now, Johnson was totally amenable, but Yarborough would not ride in the car with Johnson." The president, Kenny noted, was outraged.

"That is just stupid," Jack snapped. "Make it happen," he ordered Kenny.

And of course, as he had done so many times in the past, Kenny did just that, made it happen. He enlisted the Speaker of the House, Albert Thomas, a longtime Kennedy ally, to help him knock some heads together. Thomas was delighted to join in the fray. Thomas, the long-serving congressman from Houston, born in Nacogdoches, Texas, in 1898, became a student of politics and had run and won the House seat for the eighth district, when then Congressman Joe Eagle decided to run for Senate. Thomas became a protégé of Lyndon Johnson's, though unlike Johnson, Thomas was generally conservative, which largely reflected the Houston political area. But he was a tough contender. He was the kind of man that Kenny and Jack called "a politician's politician."

Both Jack and Kenny had grown to like and respect his tough-minded approach to politics, never mind how much bacon he delivered for the state of Texas. He had become a ruthless politician who was owed many favors across the state and in Congress. Kenny figured, given his history with Lyndon, he was just the fellow to enlist to knock a few heads together, specifically Yarborough and Connally, who were both deeply in political debt to the wily Thomas.

Kenny said later with a chuckle:

We got them to work it, but only after Connally agreed to invite Yarborough to the house party. Yarborough agreed to do that and invite the whole congressional delegation. Just crazy, but it all had worked out by the time we landed at Love Field. Johnson and Yarborough agreed to ride together. We were all going to go to Austin together and then to the dinner. Everything was smoothed over. Everybody was invited to Connally's house and it was then all fine. But it had been a tough, tough fight to work it out. Congressman Thomas and I sat with Connally for twenty-five minutes trying to push Connally. In the end, it was Thomas who had put the thing together and got it solved. Therefore, everything had been solved when we went and arrive at Love Field in Dallas on Air Force One.

However, Johnson had very little influence on it. He was willing to do anything we wanted, but, of course, typical Johnson, we had to push him to cooperate because he really did not want to get involved. Truthfully, in our view, both the president and I felt that Johnson had in fact sulked, as usual, through the whole trip.

The political fight between Yarborough and Connally seemed so stupid and irrelevant now. Jack was dead. Murdered. And John Connally, well, he was fighting for his life at Parkland Hospital. Nodding silently to a Johnson aide who passed him wordlessly, Kenny remembered the way they had gotten out of Parkland with the president's body and shook his head as he made his way back to Jackie and Dave.

For a while Kenny thought that he, Jackie, and Dave might end up in a Dallas jail. After all, they had broken Texas law. He had, in the law's eyes, stolen Jack's body. According to Texas law, the president's body should have remained in Texas for an official autopsy, but Kenny and Jackie had no intention of allowing that to happen:

> Now we get to the plane and we are all punchy and numb. I am concerned that the Dallas police are going to come and take the president's body off the plane. They could have and by law had a right to do so, but we had no idea what was going on and had no intention of leaving the president's body in their care. So we had forced our way, forced our way out of the hospital and through police lines with the president's body.
>
> Jackie Kennedy is falling apart at this stage. She is covered in blood and brains, her husband has been murdered in front of her. She is in shock, rambling and not making sense. She is worried about her children and at one point as we got on the plane with the body of the president, as I told Bobby later, I honestly thought she was going to have a heart attack right in my arms. I needed to get her some place where I prayed she could gather herself.
>
> Frankly, I am petrified that having just lost the president, who is my responsibility, I am now going to lose his wife. She's got two kids. How I am going to explain this to Bobby? This is my responsibility. I failed. So, we get on the plane and I am urging Godfrey to get the pilot to take off. The Dallas police could be here any moment. They could pull their patrol cars in front of the plane and block our take-off or, even more frightening given the threats exchanged at Parkland Hospital, they could very well shoot out the tires of the plane to stop us from taking off with the president's body. My fear is they will shoot out the tires, board the plane, guns drawn, pull off the president's body in front of Jackie, who would have had that heart attack. I am the one in the wrong here, not the Dallas police, remember. I am the

one who took the president's body by force out of Parkland and it was against Texas state law. Time is of the essence; we've got to get off the ground. My heart is pounding and that is all I can think of just now. Let's get the hell out of here.

Godfrey McHugh ran up to the pilot, our pilot, we thought, and said, "Kenny wants you to take off! What is the delay?" Well, we did not know Johnson was on the plane. We are on Air Force Two and we thought he was gone with Air Force One. In the rush, we did not even remember seeing Air Force Two sitting there.

Now, Godfrey comes running back and tells us that this is not Air Force Two, but Air Force One. This can only mean Johnson is on the plane. This is the first time we realized that we were are even on Air Force One! What the hell is he still doing here? We agreed he would leave for Washington, DC, immediately.

Godfrey then told me that he had told the pilot to take off, and was told by one of Johnson's men, "Tell O'Donnell he is not the Commander in Chief anymore. His president is dead." Well, I'm stunned. Godfrey is shocked. He comes back and tells me this and tells me we are on Air Force One, so that has to mean President Johnson is on the plane.

I was stunned at the language. Who would say something like to me? Mac Kilduff. That's who. He is the press secretary who I fired the day before. Against my better judgment, I had agreed he could complete the Texas trip and then he was to clear out. Well, the new president does not know he has been fired. Why would he? He was vice president an hour ago. So [Kilduff] is up with President Johnson trying to ingratiate himself and see if he can keep his job, because, he figures correctly, I am out. But this is the first I know the president is on the plane.

Lady Bird recalled:

> The casket was in the back hallway of the plane. At first
> Lyndon and I did not even realize it was there and that they—
> Kenny, Jackie and Dave—had somehow gotten it on the
> plane. I went back to see Mrs. Kennedy and she was sitting
> there with her husband's casket and her dress was stained
> with blood. One leg was almost entirely covered with it and
> her right glove was caked—that immaculate woman—it was
> caked with blood—her husband's blood. Somehow it was the
> most poignant sight—exquisitely dressed and caked in blood.
> I asked her if I could help her change? She said, Oh no. Thank
> you, I am fine. I will change later. And then she said a lot of
> things, some I didn't understand. And then something—if,
> with a person that gentle, that dignified, you can say had an
> element of fierceness, she said, "I want them to see what they
> have done to Jack." I did not know how to reply.

With Jackie safely sitting with Lady Bird, Dave, and the president's casket, Kenny got up. He admittedly said later that he
was "confused":

> I got up and went up front to see if I can find out what is
> happening. I also wanted to leave Lady Bird and Jackie a
> moment to speak. But still, I just knew we needed to get off
> the ground. If necessary, I will take care of Kilduff person-
> ally and take charge. I knew I was prepared to do what had
> to be done. Come on, I am thinking as I walk, wheels up for
> Christ's sake and let's go before Jackie has a heart attack and
> the cops arrive and try to take the body off. I have no sense
> that if that happened, that Johnson would stand up to them.
> He seems completely focused on this swearing-in ceremony,
> not Jackie, not the fear of conspiracy. Just nuts. I decided

first to go see Lyndon. I went in to see the new president. I walked in and he gets up, gives me a hug.

Kenny, not an outwardly emotional man, did not know how to respond. He stood there motionless, hands at his side. In all the years he had known Jack, even at some very emotional moments, such as the morning of November 8, outside on the lawn at Bobby's house at Hyannis Port, when both Kenny and he knew they had achieved their dream and Jack had won, at that very emotional moment neither man had spoken. Instead, Jack simply reached out and squeezed Kenny's shoulder. From both men's viewpoint, that gesture spoke volumes and was all that had to be said at the time.

Johnson released Kenny from his bear-like embrace and placed a hand on each shoulder, bringing Kenny forcefully back to the present.

"Before I can say anything," Kenny recalled, "he says he talked to Bobby. Bobby told him he ought to be and has to be sworn in right there on the plane, before he leaves Love Field, and this must be done in order to become president. Well, I am even more confused now. I am trying to remember my constitutional history at this point while Johnson is talking. I am standing thinking, wait a minute, the minute the president was declared dead, Johnson became president. It is automatic. You don't ever have to be sworn in. I am thinking to myself, Jesus, Bobby must know this. What the hell is he thinking?"

In truth, of course, Bobby never said it, which Kenny found out later that night at the White House when he and Bobby finally got a moment to speak alone and Bobby asked Kenny, "What the hell happened?":

Bobby got angry, because he didn't understand. When Lyndon called, he is in shock. He didn't know the background either of what had happened in Dallas. He had been trying to reach me, but had been unsuccessful. Now he is being blamed for everything. He got mad. I don't blame him. I am sure when Lyndon called to ask what the law was, Bobby just threw the phone to somebody. Bobby is sitting stunned at the pool at Hickory Hill, it's not like he has a law book sitting there. Later Bobby admitted he did not even remember the conversation. In the end, it was all unnecessary.

Johnson simply wanted to be sworn in as president in Texas. Now, there is nothing wrong with that. Why not just say it? You are president now. You can do whatever the hell you want, except if you have a conspiracy you ought to be up in the airplane and on your way to Washington. But, you know, that is not my business. He is president. I don't work for him. Essentially, the man I work for is dead. I don't have a job here anymore, so it is his call. I thought it was a mistake, but he is president now. He can do whatever the hell he wants. He does not have to care what Ken O'Donnell thinks anymore. That's just politics.

Honestly, I was just concerned about Jackie. I really was worried about Jackie and wanted to get her to Bobby. I just could not face Bobby if something happened to her. It was bad enough that I had to face him about the president.

Johnson explained to Kenny that since Bobby had insisted he be sworn in before leaving Texas, they were waiting for his friend, Judge Sarah Hughes, to arrive. Kenny was stunned.

"Mr. President," Kenny said, forcing himself to mouth the words, "that is not possible. It is not a good idea after what Jackie has been through."

The mental picture of Jackie covered in her husband's blood and brains was still fresh on his mind.

Lyndon looked puzzled. "She said she wanted to be here," he explained.

Kenny was confused. It did not sound like Jackie. When could they have spoken? Still, as Lyndon spoke, Kenny looked past him and out the window of the plane, looking across at the tarmac. Time was of the essence; the Dallas police could be here any moment. He did not have time to argue the point—he needed to talk to Jackie.

"I am thinking to myself—and I say this to Dave later—my thinking was, Look, if these Dallas cops show up, they can put a motorcycle in front of Air Force One, shoot out the tires, and take the body under the law in Texas. We broke the law by removing his body. I am still not sure what we are dealing with. Let's go."

Though Johnson was still speaking, Kenny was no longer listening. All he could think of was the cops arriving, having an awful scene, and Jackie having a heart attack. He debated whether or not he should tell the new president what they had done, that they had broken Texas law and stolen Jack's body at gunpoint from Parkland Hospital. They were now on the run from the police.

Kenny later told Bobby:

In retrospect, I realized if I had told Lyndon what we had done, he would have acted. It would have been wheels up immediately. But I didn't because I had just broken the law in the new president's own state. I felt telling him would put him in a terrible position. You would then be asking him, you know, Mr. President, your first act as the new president is to break the law in Texas. It just politically would have been a disaster for him. I just could not put him in that position. I did not know him at that time, certainly not as well as I knew Jack, so I could not take the chance. This had been my decision, I realized that. I would have to bear the responsibility and the potential legal consequences. I could not involve the new president.

With that in mind, Kenny, sick with worry, said nothing to Lyndon about the reason for speed.

"Look," Kenny said to Bobby that night, "the Texas cops don't know what's happening. Who knows what they are going to do. I didn't want to find out. The scene at the hospital was bad enough. I didn't want to find out. This is not what I want you to have to deal with."

Bobby shook his head. "I never told him to stay there and be sworn in," Bobby insisted. "Never."

Later, Kenny would admit that Bobby's recollection of the conversation he had with Lyndon over the swearing-in issue was cloudy:

Given the shock of the situation and the shock of the news Bobby had just received about his brother's murder, his memory of what happened next is hazy. He even admitted later, "It . . . can't be relied on completely." I would not swear by Bobby's recollection of the conversation. Remember, Bobby is in total shock now. I reconstructed it in my own mind that the president called Bobby to extend sympathy, tell him what happened, and frankly get his legal view. I don't know who would be so stupid to suggest the president call Bobby, the murdered president's brother, with such a question. I suspect it was Homer Thornberry grandstanding. It was stupid. Both men are in shock right now. Johnson was president the minute they declared John Kennedy dead. He is president of the United States with all the powers of the presidency. I know that from high school civics class. There was no need for the call to Bobby. He never had to be sworn in.

President Johnson said to me, as I recall, "Bobby says I have to be sworn in." I was stunned. It made no sense and I said, which was not my place, but I said, "Bobby said this?" He hedges and says, "Well, Bobby put Deputy Attorney General Nick Katzenbach on." I was confused even more then. Katzenbach? What the hell is he doing talking to Katzenbach? Course calling Bobby was stupid. Bobby would not have the slightest idea. None.

It would take some time and distance for Kenny to understand that in the end, Johnson had made a brilliant political decision. With his well-tuned political instincts, Johnson understood an essential point now being overlooked by the Kennedy New Frontiersmen in their despair.

"The country, the people needed to see Lyndon Johnson sworn in. They needed to see for themselves that ever so important transfer of power so that Johnson could convey to the nation as a whole, despite the murder of President Kennedy, that the country was in his hands, he was in control, and that there was indeed an orderly transfer of power," Kenny said later.

On Air Force One, Johnson's voice brought Kenny back to the present. "Kenny," Lyndon said, moving uncomfortably close, "would you ask Mrs. Kennedy to come stand here with me while I get sworn in?"

Kenny just stared, again stunned at the request. "I couldn't believe it," Kenny told Bobby later. "I said, 'Mr. President, you can't do that. That poor little kid has had enough for one day. To stand here and hear that oath that she heard a few years ago with her husband at her side. You can't do that Mr. President.' He just stared at me. Now, I am completely confused. When did he talk to her? She's never left the president's body and I have been with her the whole time, except when she went to the ladies' room, because I was worried about her well-being."

"Why would I make that up, Kenny?" Johnson asked, puzzled and perhaps a bit hurt. "You are just in shock still," Johnson said, perhaps to cover his hurt and Kenny's bad manners, again putting his hands on Kenny's shoulders. "Now you just go get Mrs. Kennedy for me, would you? The judge is here and we can get this done."

Kenny said nothing. He shook his head and turned and retreated to find Jackie, who now was in Lyndon's cabin with the door closed. Dave explained to Kenny she wanted to freshen up before facing Johnson and the ceremony. Dave had no idea when Jackie had talked to Johnson either. He was, he explained to Kenny, as surprised as was Kenny at the turn of events. With time ticking away, Kenny paced liked a caged tiger, back and forth, outside her room, growing increasingly agitated.

"I was waiting for her to come out," Kenny would later tell his wife Helen, recounting the day's horrendous events. "I wanted to get this done, so I don't get her arrested, never mind everything else. I did not break in. You don't break into a girl's bedroom or bathroom very often, especially not the wife of the President of the United States. I was not the kind of fellow who would just go barging into her room under the best of circumstances, never mind now. Finally, I paced up and down for five minutes and I am now hysterical. Finally, I had to, I just walked in."

The sight that greeted him was bizarre. Jackie was sitting combing her hair. She sat staring the mirror with a blank expression as she combed her hair. Kenny assumed she was just going through the motions, still too much in shock to respond to anything.

Having run out of time and feeling as though she seemed oblivious to his presence, Kenny finally interrupted her. "I said, 'Do you want to go out there? He said you do. You do not have to do this if you do not want to.' 'Yes,' she said, to my surprise, 'I think I ought to. Jack would want me to. I owe that much to the country.'"

Kenny was surprised. Johnson did talk to her. "I don't know when," Kenny admitted, "but he had asked her and she did indeed agree. I didn't know that till she told me." As she rose to go, Kenny held open the door, and Jackie suddenly stopped. "Kenny," she said, "should I change?" Kenny looked at her. There she is, he thought, covered in her husband's blood and brains.

After a moment, Kenny said simply, "No, Mrs. Kennedy. You look fine."

She nodded and walked past him. He began to follow her up the passageway. In truth, maybe she should have changed, he thought as he walked behind, noticing even the back of her stockings and skirt were covered in Jack's blood.

"But, again," Kenny recalled, "I am thinking the cops could be here any minute; I do not want anything that will delay this swearing in. We go up. I stand beside her. He takes the oath. The photo gets taken. The plane takes off and we are finally, thank God, up in the air."

With the ceremony completed, Kenny and Jackie retreated to join Dave for the return to Washington. As they returned to their seats, Dave poured the drinks.

"Yes," Jackie said, taking hers, "I think after that we all need this." Kenny took his and slowly lowered himself into his seat next to Jackie. The day's events had yet to fully sink in. All he knew for sure now, as he felt Air Force One reach cruising speed, was that they were safely off the ground and headed out of Texas airspace.

They sat in silence, the only noise the soft roar of Air Force One's engines. Just then Kenny heard a voice. It was Johnson aide Bill Moyers: "The president would like to speak with you again." Kenny sat with his eyes closed for a moment. Maybe it was all a bad dream, maybe when he opened his eyes it would be his president, his friend Jack, who wanted to speak with him. Kenny held his eyes shut, not wanting to open them, when he heard the voice again, "Kenny?" Kenny opened his eyes. Jackie and Dave were staring at him. Kenny turned; the casket was still there.

"Tell the president I am coming," Kenny said, slowly getting up, putting down his drink, and squeezing Jackie's shoulder as he passed her—just as Jack had done with him so many times. "I will be right back, kid." She nodded.

"Please hurry, Kenny," was all she said.

Kenny rose and followed Moyers back to Lyndon's room. "He had asked to see me and he used the famous line he used with every staff member, though at the time I did not know it, and it got me through."

Lyndon looked at Kenny and began immediately. "I need you now more than he did," he said while changing his shirt. "Ken, I need to you stay. You can't leave me. You are the only one of them I get along with there. I don't know one soul in that group—don't trust them. I don't know all those big city fellas. My staff does not know anything about those people past the Mason-Dixon line. They don't know anything."

Later, Kenny admitted he was only half listening. He wanted to get back to Jackie. "I was still in shock. I was noncommittal at that moment. I wanted to stay with Jackie, and if I had said yes to him then, that would mean I could not do that. I felt if I said yes at that moment, I'd have to be with him. I was still in shock, and my job, as I saw it, was to get Jackie to Bobby. Once that is done, I can answer his question. In truth, at the very moment, I simply could not answer him."

Kenny retreated and sat with Jackie. "The longest conversation with any of the Johnson people, that I recollect," Kenny later told Bobby, "was that Bill Moyers came back and said,

'We're going to have a meeting with the NSC and the president would like you to be there.'"

Jackie stared at Kenny. While saying nothing, her eyes implored him to stay. He understood without her saying a word. "I said to Moyers, 'Bill, I don't have the stomach for it. I just don't.'"

Kenny admitted later on that "at this stage, I am doubtful I will stay on and so I feel this is one last mission for John Kennedy is to get him and his widow back to Washington.

"I said to Moyers, 'I can't leave her,'" nodding towards Jackie.

Moyers nodded and left, later returning to tell Kenny: "Fine. The boss understands completely, but just really, when we get back to Washington, he needs to sit down with you immediately about next steps."

Kenny said fine.

"I really had not made a commitment to stay on with Lyndon, but either way it was not the time for such a discussion. In the end," Kenny recalled, "I never said yes or no; he just assumed. Johnson said to me, 'We need to finish what he started.' So I stayed."

It was Dave Powers, Kenny noted, who "may have saved our sanity on the long, sad flight back to Washington. Maybe Lyndon deserves some credit for letting us be by ourselves with the president's [body] and simply grieve. Given the situation, he could have demanded, and maybe should have, that I be with him in the NSC meetings and so forth, but he allowed me to stay with Jackie and Jack. That was where I needed to be at that time, for me as much as for her."

Dave, Jack's favorite Irish storyteller, stayed true to his reputation, regaling Jackie and Kenny with funny stories of Jack both on and off the political stage.

"For Jackie," Kenny realized, "this was a unique insight into Jack. She did not know this side of him, because this was his political personality, his business face if you will; he was very different with her in private. I came to realize this very early in my relationship with him, that he very much saw Jackie and the children as a refuge from his hectic and demanding political life. They did not talk politics; they talked literature, art, and what the children were doing. For Jackie, hearing Dave's stories was a wonderful way to meet this other side of Jack. And," Kenny added sadly, "to try to find a way for us all to cope with this thing that had just happened."

These get-togethers between Kenny, Jackie, Bobby, and Dave would continue for years. They would meet for lunch and drinks, first in Washington and then in New York. They would tell stories, laugh, and in so doing keep the spirit of Jack, as well as their sanity, alive. Kenny and Jackie in particular would grow increasingly close. She, like her husband before her, came to rely upon Kenny's protective nature, his no-nonsense, no-bull straight talk and advice.

"I know," Jackie confided later to Bobby, "that as he did with my Jack, Kenny will always have my back." This would prove true until the end of Kenny's life. He would be one of the few people to stand with her during her tumultuous marriage to Ari Onassis. With Bobby then gone, Kenny in particular would be needed for Jackie to rely upon during the onslaught brought on by her marriage to Onassis, but also to help her cope with the none-too-flattering revelations of Jack's personal life that Kenny had for so many years tried to protect her from. But that was to come. For this flight home to Washington, they were simply trying to cope.

When Air Force One touched down in Washington, the long simmering conflict between Bobby and Lyndon once again reared its ugly head, this time in a most uncomfortable manner that would only add to the feud between the two men and the growing legend. This moment, true or not, sealed each man's dislike for the other as much as anything. Much has been made of the landing at the naval base where Lyndon and Lady Bird deplaned, as expected, from the front of Air Force One. Lyndon then made a critical and indeed deeply moving address to a shattered nation and world. But behind the scenes there was nothing but chaos.

A newsreel from the time period shows Bobby Kennedy charging up the front steps of Air Force One, then the president's body being taken off the back of the plane accompanied by his widow—still wearing her bloodstained pink suit—and Bobby, Kenny, and Dave. They then try, unsuccessfully at first, to get in the hearse to take Jack to Bethesda Naval Hospital. This is what the cameras caught, what the public saw: the Kennedys and Jack's Irish Brotherhood coming out of the back with Jack's body; Lyndon Johnson, the successor, alone with his wife at the front of Air Force One.

"Never did Lyndon ask anyone about getting off the plane with Jack's body and Jackie. Never. I was there the whole time," Kenny reminded everyone later. "If he had asked to deplane with the First Lady and join Jackie, Bobby, me, and the president's body as we deplaned, we would have had no problem with that. In fact, we would have welcomed it, but at the time we were so focused on getting Jack's body off, we did not think of it ourselves, nor did he ask." Furthermore, Kenny maintained, Bobby's arrival on the scene also changed their focus. "I don't know who ever suggested or said to them, Lyndon would like to get off with us, but it never got communicated to us. That is not true. He never asked."

Eventually, Jackie's chosen chronicler of her Dallas experience (and later nemesis), author William Manchester, makes a big scene of it, as did author Jim Bishop, who Kenny said "does worse":

Of course in my view, Jackie never should have talked to Manchester or Bishop, but that is a different story. Bishop in particular was nasty and frankly simply wrong. He says that all the Kennedy people crowded around the body and snuck it out the back while Lyndon was speaking, all done in an effort to deny Lyndon the opportunity to deplane with Jackie and the president's body. That's bull. Who are all the Kennedy people? There were only three of us on the plane. Jackie, Dave, and me. The rest were Johnson people. And the body could only be taken off one way. He knew that.

What happened really was the soldiers got on and brought the ramp up. We were going to go out front, and then I said, I don't know why, I said, I think we ought to leave with him. We came with him. We ought to leave with him. Frankly, I see this as my final act of service to my president and the country. I had no intention of staying on. This is my final act. It was really a moment of emotion for me. My final duty to John Fitzgerald Kennedy, my president and my friend, whom I feel I had let down, the least I could do is accompany his body off the plane one last time. It is the least I can do. My last act.

Jackie got emotional and she agreed, as did Dave. And Bobby was, of course, already a mess. Remember, this is the first time Bobby has seen Jack in the casket and seen his body. While we had had some time to adjust and process, Bobby had none, so he is a mess. He agreed. So, we all grabbed the body and told the soldiers we would meet them down on the runway with the body. It was really just an emotional Irish moment, where our emotions took over. We were not even thinking about President Johnson or the press or cameras. Dammit, we carried him on the plane and we will carry him off. We don't even know where Johnson is, and I am assuming he has gotten off.

Bobby had come through the plane. He is a hysterical mess. I asked him if he saw Lyndon? He shook his head and said, No. Well, of course later as it turns out, Lyndon had been on the plane when Bobby got on and had put his hand out to greet Bobby and Bobby had, according to Lyndon, just pushed past him without word as if he did not exist.

Look, I am sure that is true. Bobby was in shock and wanted to get to Jackie. Was it rude? Sure. Was against protocol to simply shove the President of the United States aside? Sure. But remember, his brother has just been murdered. We don't know what is going on. He is wondering if his actions helped get his brother killed. He desperately wanted to get to Jackie. There is no textbook for this; we just were doing the best could for Jack and Jackie. As his Irish Brotherhood, we still felt this last act—Jack was still the president.

Once Bobby and Jackie had pulled themselves together, Kenny told Bobby what they wanted to do and why:

Bobby is an emotional Irish fellow. He agreed with us. He is crying now. We all are. He took Jackie's arm. Dave and I grabbed the body and we got off. We had no idea all the press and cameras were there or we might have thought twice. We assumed the press would follow Johnson. We were stunned. We get off and all these cameras and flashes in our faces as we carry the body to the ambulance. The press just crowded in with nobody to hold them back. It was frightening.

To make it worse, the damn back door of the ambulance is locked, so we cannot get in and we have to stand there with the body till they unlock it. Stupid. Just a series of things. I never heard anybody say, nor did he say it to me, that the president wants to deplane with the body. Never. I only read about that afterward. That is all made up. I don't believe Johnson made that request. His focus, as it should be, is on the country, he is not looking for press hits here. He is still in shock himself. We never argued. There were no fights. Moyers was there, he was our friend. Jack Valenti was there. I thought he worked for Albert Thomas. We did not know these people. Why would be fighting with them?

We all in different ways were simply trying to cope with a horrific event and the new reality that event brought to all our lives. Jackie, Bobby, Dave, and I were focused on one thing, and one thing only, that was to bring Jack home. Right or wrong, that was all we cared about at that moment.

It was, in their view, the last act in Jack's political life and in the lives of the Irish Brotherhood that had seen him from Bowdoin Street in Boston in 1946 to the White House in 1961 and, fatefully, to Dallas in 1963.

"Our focus," Kenny said, "our last act that night, was to get him home."

CHAPTER SEVEN
THE TRANSITION

Helen Sullivan O'Donnell, a slim, pretty, blue-eyed housewife was having lunch with some friends at Paul Young's at the famous Mayflower Hotel on Connecticut Avenue. She was seated at the center table. She simply loved Washington. She loved the attention, the excitement, and the fun. She delighted in the success of Jack and Bobby Kennedy. She was thrilled with all the good they had done for her family and what she and her husband believed they would and could do for the nation.

Helen had sacrificed a great deal to be here. The reality was that not one step of Jack Kennedy's climb to power had been easy for any of them. She once teased the then president-elect, only half in fun, that Kenny had not been home for ten years while Jack had climbed the political ladder to the White House. Jack had understood her sacrifice and as often as possible let her know that he deeply appreciated them. He understood Kenny's sacrifice, which was also Helen's, as she was forced by circumstances to raise five children largely on her own. Kenny was often gone, always with the president. Not even holidays mattered if Jack needed him, which was often and always.

Helen told her gal pals that this had been the happiest time in their lives. She could not even remember what she was eating or what they talked about that day. All she recalled was the waiter rushing towards her, his face ashen, still grasping a flask of water to refill some forgotten glasses. For some reason, she remembered the water splashing as he ran towards her and she remembered thinking, how clumsy of him.

There had been shooting in Dallas, he practically shouted at her. The president had been hit, but so had Kenny since he was ever present at Jack's side. The only thing she was to recall later was how loud the silence had been in the dining room. She remembered feeling for a moment as though she could not breathe.

Helen told friends that at that moment she felt as though she was falling down a black hole and could not save herself. Maybe, she said later, she never did get back to the spot in which she had first fallen. Perhaps none of them did.

The news of Kenny being hit turned out to be wrong, but not all wounds can be seen. Helen came to realize that while Kenny had not been physically injured in Dallas, he nevertheless returned emotionally wounded. He was unable to forgive himself for not saving the president. In the end, he could not shake a sense of failure.

The new president seemed to grasp, or at least understand, Kenny's pain. He would often call Helen in the interim period before Kenny returned to work at the White House. He was calling to check in on Helen and Kenny, to "help in any way I can," he said. As time went on and Kenny had yet to return to the White House and his job, Johnson grew frustrated. At one point he asked Helen, "What's wrong with him? He's gotta get back to work."

She replied, "You see, Mr. President, not all wounds can be seen, but are still nevertheless just as fatal."

Change had come to all of their lives, no matter how much they all wished circumstances had been different, he pointed out to her. "We all have got to get back to work," he added. "I need Kenny here."

He was right, of course, but in the end it took a call from Bobby to get Kenny to walk back through the White House gates.

"Jack would want you to do what you could," Bobby told Kenny, despite the fact that he himself had not yet been able to walk through the doors of the Justice Department.

"I just knew we needed Kenny in there with Lyndon to protect Jack's legacy. He had to go back," Bobby said.

Kenny went to work.

As he stood outside the White House gates that morning, he found he could not walk through. His legs felt frozen. His driver, the same military man who had driven him for the past three years, was surprised when Kenny had asked to be let off just outside of the White House gates. But despite his promises to his wife and Bobby, he was having trouble taking the next step.

"It was nothing personal, really, in terms of Lyndon Johnson," Kenny explained. "I just guess I was not mentally prepared for that change. Dallas and the events were still ringing in my ears."

Kenny decided, not for the first time, to turn and make the cold lonely walk to Arlington. As he did so he found himself wondering about the events in Dallas, the decisions he made and ones he might have made that could have changed the outcome.

From there he began to wonder about Oswald and what the story was. Lyndon had told him on the telephone the evening before that he wanted to discuss his plans for the Warren Commission with him. Maybe just that thought alone was what was compelling him at the break of dawn to be walking towards Arlington instead of into the Oval Office. He kept his head down as he walked, staring at the pavement as if he might learn something. In truth, it was a way to avoid making eye contact with the many passersby heading toward the White House and downtown Washington while he walked the opposite way.

His mind wandered to his last conversations with President Kennedy about the Texas trip. He remembered it was Tuesday, just two days before the trip and it was a busy day in the Kennedy White House. Kenny was busily involved in last-minute preparations for the trip, the usual visitors and the last-minute items Jack wanted to accomplish before he and Jackie left for Texas. "The White House correspondents were giving Pierre Salinger a hard time because I had refused to allow him to release the specific street routes the president's motorcade would follow on his visits to cities on the Texas tour. But the Secret Service had advised me not give out such specific information in advance of the trip because of the rough treatment of Adlai Stevenson by the crowd in Dallas when he visited there for a United Nations Day ceremony on October 24. They felt the events had made it advisable to take precautions against any planned demonstrations."

On that Tuesday, President Kennedy had a long meeting with Dean Rusk focused mostly on Vietnam. Rusk and others were leaving the next day for a trip to Hawaii and Japan. Once there, Rusk planned to meet with Ambassador Henry Cabot Lodge, Kennedy's man in Vietnam, to get a sense of the Vietnam situation. From there Rusk and several cabinet members would go on to Tokyo for a meeting with the Japanese on economic issues. Part of Rusk's job was to pave the way for

Kennedy's own planned trip to Japan during his tour of the Far East. Jackie was going with him and she had been busily reading up on Japan and other countries so that she might be well prepared for the trip, as she had been in 1962.

After he talked with Rusk, the president called Kenny in to his office:

> He explained that he and Jackie were considering moving the departure of their trip to Japan, the Philippines, India, and Pakistan forward to a date shortly after New Year's. Kennedy said, "Let's move it to right after New Year's Day. Right after we get back from Texas you go out there and advance the trip. You could do it in about a month. You'll be gone during December, not a bad thing for you to be away then because it is quiet here at Christmas time and one of the few times I can spare you. You could time it so you could be back the day before Christmas." I stared at him, wondering if he was joking.
>
> I said, "If I came home on the day before Christmas, after being away the whole month of December, I would come home to an empty house."
>
> "What do you mean?" he asked.
>
> "My wife Helen is a patient woman, as you know, but if I was missing before Christmas for the whole month, she'd pack up the kids and leave, Mr. President. My situation is different than yours, you don't have to do any Christmas shopping and you don't have to go out and buy the Christmas tree and put the lights on it and decorate it. You don't have to buy presents and put them together for the kids. If I were gone the two weeks before Christmas again, Helen would divorce me."

Dave chimed in on Kenny's behalf, "Mr. President, if it got

around Worcester and Massachusetts that you kept Kenny away the week before Christmas, no woman would vote for you in 1964."

The president laughed. "Oh, all right, put the advance trip off until January. But listen, are you sure I'll be leaving Texas in time to have lunch here with Henry Cabot Lodge on Sunday? He's coming all the way from Vietnam to see me and I don't want to keep him waiting. It's an important discussion we need to have."

"Don't worry about it," Kenny said to him. "It's all set."

On Sunday, he was watching the casket being carried to the rotunda of the Capitol.

By the time Kenny returned to the White House it was past ten in the morning. The place was now filled with new people, some Kenny recognized, by face anyway, some he did not. But they were all busy and moving to go somewhere. Seeing Kenny and knowing how close he was to the slain president, everyone was kind and respectful. Kenny said little and mostly nodded in return to their condolences.

By the time he reached the outer ring of the Oval Office, he really wanted to turn around again. As he stood outside the doorway to his office area, he noticed someone he did not know sitting at his desk and using the telephone. As de facto Chief of Staff for Kennedy, nothing in the White House moved without his say-so. He got there early and was nearly always there before the president came down. And he stayed late, rarely leaving the Oval Office until after he and the president had had time to catch up on the day's events. Now, as he stood in the Johnson White House, nobody noticed him.

He was just about to walk away when the door to the Oval Office opened and the new president caught sight of him.

"Kenny," he seemed to bellow, though Kenny later admitted

maybe that was being unfair. "Come on in! We were just talking about you. Some things we need to discuss."

Just then the president noticed the young man sitting at Kenny's desk. He angrily ordered him out.

Placing his hands on Kenny's shoulders and pulling him closer than Kenny appreciated, Lyndon said, "I haven't allowed one person to sit at that desk since it happened. That's Kenny's desk, I tell them. We've all been just waiting for you."

With that, President Johnson walked into the Oval Office. Kenny followed carefully behind. He very much doubted that they had all been waiting for his return and he further doubted that they had been just talking about him or, frankly, needed him very much. As he stood across from the president, he looked around. He shuddered for a moment. The rocking chair was gone and all traces of John Fitzgerald Kennedy's presence was eliminated save the photo behind Lyndon. Cape Cod was replaced with the rolling hills of Texas.

As he spoke, Kenny noticed something else about Lyndon, something he had glimpsed briefly on that flight back to Washington on Air Force One. The tentative, unsure man who had been an unhappy and at times difficult vice president was gone. Just as it had when John Kennedy won the presidency in November 1960, the office had descended upon him.

Now, as he stood listening to Johnson describe his plans for a new approach to the civil rights bill that he wanted to push forward "for him, for our president," Kenny noticed that Lyndon Johnson was no longer the unhappy fellow of a few months ago. He was now president and everything about his demeanor made that clear. He exuded power and strength. And while Kenny would have given anything to not have had this happen—and he was quite sure Lyndon felt the same— he marveled at this country. A beloved president murdered, a transition of power to a new man, a new president, and not a shot in anger save the tragedy itself.

It was something that John Kennedy, as a student of history, would have so deeply appreciated, he thought.

Kenny took the drink and the seat the new president offered. He heard Lyndon say something about Martin King and Bobby calling him to get everyone on board with the bill. Kenny sipped his drink and tried to shake himself loose and remember where he was, to focus on the present, not the past. He tried and failed to explain that he thought Bobby was still deeply grieving and likely not much help just now. But he agreed to call him, as the president asked.

But as he listened, he realized this was all going to be a hell of lot harder than he thought. Though he heard the Texas drawl speaking and the new president was certainly saying all the right things, in his mind he could still hear Jack Kennedy's voice describing the presidency: "Well, I find the work of the presidency rewarding. I believe in the Greek definition of happiness. It is the full use of your powers along the lines of excellence. I find therefore that presidency provides some happiness."

While that had been a sentiment Kenny had certainly shared with John Kennedy, he was not at all sure that was true, at least for him, anymore.

CHAPTER EIGHT
MAKING THEM ALL "JOHNSON MEN"

As Air Force One had headed back to Washington, Kenny had made one last call—or so he believed at the time—in his role as chief of staff. He called the White House and ordered the Oval Office stripped, packed up, and moved out so that the vice president's things could be moved in. He also ordered boxes and boxes of John Kennedy's papers and documents sealed and moved to his home at 5720 Massachusetts Avenue. He and Bobby would decide later what to do, but he did not want the new president to see the documents first. He explained this decision only to Bobby. Kenny and Bobby agreed that the documents would have to be gone through and decisions made. Some of them would eventually be given to the Kennedy Library, some destroyed, and others given to Jackie. But at the moment nobody had the stomach for it.

They were quietly placed in the basement along with the flags from the Oval Office and Kenny's dreams of the world Jack might have created. That was gone now. At some moments it still felt like a bad dream. Kenny's younger sister Justine, who worked for Dick Maguire, the treasurer at the Democratic National Committee, said they all got through those first months—the funeral and the holidays—as if they were zombies. Kenny said, "Every morning when the alarm went off I would open my eyes and think it was all a bad dream, but of course it was not. It was painfully real." Kenny, Helen, Bobby, and Jackie were left to pick up the pieces of their shattered hopes.

Still, despite there being a new president, the Kennedy presidency was in many ways still in operation. Johnson understood this at some level. For the thousand days of his vice presidency, he had felt like the outsider, the interloper who was treated with unvarnished contempt for not being a "Kennedy Man" earlier and for being at odds with Bobby. On three different occasions Jack Kennedy had called Kenny into his office and ordered him to remind the White House staff and the Kennedy people spread throughout the government that they were to treat Johnson properly and as befitting the office of vice president, or they would be dealt with. The fact that he felt compelled to do this on three occasions speaks volumes for how poorly Johnson was treated.

But that was then, this was now. Lyndon Johnson had now become president, and the Oval Office, where he said he felt he had stood naked and stripped of all power and dignity— that office now belonged to him. The Kennedy rocker was out, the Texas longhorn was in. Lyndon was determined to take the reins of power with dignity and compassion, he told others. "I will treat those men as they should have treated me. I will make them Johnson men." The task that lay before him was daunting to any man, but Lyndon summoned all his courage, banished for now the insipid fear and insecurity that had haunted his life, and took the reins of power with clarity of purpose.

Johnson later tried to explain his approach in terms best

understood by the Texas ranchers that he had known all his life: "Everything was in chaos. We were all spinning around and around, trying to come to grips with what had happened, but the more we tried to understand it, the more confused we got. We were like a bunch of cattle caught in a swamp, unable to move in either direction simply going 'round and round'; I understood that, I knew what had to be done. There is but one way to get the cattle out of the swamp. And that is for a man on a horse to take the lead, to assume command, to provide direction. In that period of confusion, after the assassination, I was that man."

While Lyndon certainly understood the pain felt by Jackie, Bobby, and the men around the slain president, he was now president and he had a country to run. Whatever doubts or fears he might have had had to be pushed into the background. He had noticed that Kennedy's office had been stripped and was not happy, but he said nothing to Kenny in those early days after the murder in Dallas. Instead, he put it on his mental list of perceived slights from the Kennedys, more specifically from Bobby.

Later Johnson would tell Kenny, "Bobby Kennedy may not be happy I am here. But the thing is done. We are where we are now. The country—no, the world—was looking to me and I have to respond with strength and determination. I had not wished to be here, I had not planned to be here, but I am here now."

Johnson was president of the United States and he planned to use his position to carry on the legacy of John Kennedy as best he could. It was what Kenny wanted to hear, but of course Lyndon had more in mind, much more, but he was not comfortable sharing that with Kenny yet. He needed Kenny and the Kennedy men to stay on board for both personal and political reasons, but he never saw himself as being their intimate in the way Kennedy had been. Lyndon knew he had to use the Kennedy legacy and he hated to describe it that way, but he had to keep the country focused and convinced that while he had inherited Kennedy's mantle, he saw it as just that—Kennedy's mantle. "The presidency," Johnson explained, "is more than about me, it is about this awesome country. My job is to be the president for all the people."

As he saw it, the Kennedy men were Kennedy's "Irish Mafia," led by Kenny O'Donnell. These men were Kennedy's personal friends—O'Donnell, O'Brien, Maguire, and others brought on with them. These were Kennedy's men: Harvard professors, labor leaders, the Kennedy cabinet, the White House technicians, big-city politicians. Keeping them in place was in no small manner a way to keep Bobby Kennedy off his back and the country squarely behind him. He saw Bobby as his biggest threat to his power. In or out of office, Bobby was the immediate heir to the Kennedy legacy. With John Kennedy's death Bobby had assumed, like it or not, the mantle of the Kennedy family and the Democratic Party. In Lyndon's mind that could only mean trouble.

Lyndon believed it when he told Kenny over drinks that evening in December that Bobby now had the mantle of leadership for the family and the party. "Mr. President," Kenny said, his voice tinged with sadness, "like you, Bobby would much rather have President Kennedy here and things be as they had been. He is just trying to get through this right now. I assure you he has no other ambitions than the well-being of his family and Jackie and the children."

Lyndon sipped his drink and let the moment sit for a second. It was unlike him, but given the horrendous manner in which had come to this office, he was determined to put the "old acrimony" between himself and Bobby behind them for as long as possible. He was working hard to do so. He assured

Kenny that he believed him. That he would do all he could to be there for the Kennedy family, most especially Jackie and Bobby. "I need Bobby more than ever," he repeated.

Kenny listened and quietly hoped that Lyndon and Bobby could overcome their past differences and, for the good of the country, get along. Maybe they would never be friends, but they could perhaps learn to play on the same team. Though in his gut, Kenny admitted to friends later, he knew it was wishful thinking: "They have this instinctive distrust and competition with each other that makes no sense." Lyndon had no doubt that in the end it would be Bobby who would break ranks, though in these early days he did not tell that to Kenny. If Bobby did publicly break with Lyndon it could well split the entire Democratic Party and his administration, setting the stage for a Republican victory in November.

It wasn't just the Kennedy men, the Democratic leaders, and the public that needed reassurance. It was the entire world. The day of the funeral, Monday, Johnson had called every governor in every state of the union to assure them that the new administration was up and running. That they were in control. Republican or Democrat, it did not matter. According to Kenny, "He warned them that without their help, confidence in the new administration, 'our whole system would go awry.'"

"Listen," Johnson would say in his distinctive drawl, "we think we have the best system. We think that where a capitalist can put up a dollar, he can get a return on it. A manager can get up early to work and with money and men he can build a better mousetrap. A laborer who is worthy of his hire stands a chance of getting attention and maybe a little profit sharing system and the highest minimum wages of any nation in the world. I am asking for your trust and your help to let us continue what he began."

This phrase was repeated again and again to every single

governor until late in the evening. Journalists Rowland Evans and Robert Novak, who had become friends of Kenny's, wrote of Johnson that week: "The Governors may have been surprised to hear these earthly Americanisms but they were strangely comforted, too. There was no uncertain stammering now, no outward sign of hesitation or the weakness they had seen when he was vice president; instead it was replaced with an obvious and deep sincerity to get on with the difficult job, and there was an atmosphere of confidence, *a presidential* atmosphere of latent power and decision."

Kenny had begun to agree. He had first seen glimpses of it on the plane ride back from Dallas. "The president (Kennedy) and I never saw this side of him when he was vice president," he reminded Bobby. "Your brother would be amazed and vindicated, for this is the . . . reason he had chosen Lyndon as vice president—over so many objections. Most especially mine." Bobby, for whom the pain and his own sense of guilt was still too unbearable, only mumbled a reply. He had noticed the same thing, but was not yet able to cope with the new realities of Johnson holding the office that had belonged to his brother.

Two days later, Lyndon achieved what journalists at the time called a tour de force in delivering what was without question the most important speech of his life. The words that mattered were these:

> Let us begin. . . . Our most immediate tasks are here on this hill. First, no memorial oration or eulogy could more eloquently honor President Kennedy's memory than the earliest possible passage of the civil rights bill for which he fought so long. We have talked long enough about equal rights in this country. We have talked for one hundred years or more. It is time now we write the next chapter and to

write it in the books of law. I urge you again, as I did in 1957 and again in 1960, to enact a civil rights law so we can move forward to eliminate from this nation every trace of discrimination and oppression that is based upon race or color.

And second, no act of ours could more fittingly continue the work of President Kennedy than the early passage of the tax bill for which he fought for all this year . . . This is no time for delay. It is time for action.

In the end, Johnson reached out to appeal to the nation's hope and faith for a better future:

Let us put an end to the teaching of and preaching of hate and evil and violence. Let us turn away from the fanatics of the far left and far right, from the apostles of bigotry, from those defiant of law and those who pour venom into the nation's bloodstream . . . So let here resolve that John Fitzgerald Kennedy did not live or die in vain.

Sander Vanocur, then with NBC news as their White House correspondent, noted that by the time Lyndon Johnson had completed his speech to Congress on November 27, "he had won over many who until then had stood back, refusing to trust him." Evans and Novak noted much the same: "He had gained the confidence not only of the nation, but of those liberals who had always found him suspect and distrusted him. He had even gone out of his way to reach out to former foes such as Joseph Rauh, of the Americans for Democratic Action, even inviting his arch foe upon Air Force one to attend Senator Lehman's funeral in New York City."

Johnson was pulling together as many of the Kennedy liberal politicians and Kennedy men he could. He believed this was essential to move forward with his agenda and bring the nation together in support of his policies. His campaign to bring Kenny over began in earnest after that November speech.

In December he invited Kenny for drinks at the White House. "It is important, Kenny," Lyndon told him, "for you all to stay. If any of you leave it will tell the country that you have a problem with Lyndon Johnson and that could doom Jack's agenda in the Senate and the party at the polls in November." Those in government had to be persuaded to stay on board. If they did not, the people would draw the clear and obvious conclusion that these Kennedy men choose not to work for Johnson. "You would not be putting just me in a difficult spot, but you would jeopardize his agenda, which I am determined to force through Congress, especially civil rights, which would be his lasting legacy."

Johnson was appealing to Kenny's love of Jack, his love of party and country. After all, both men knew Johnson was correct. "It was just," Kenny explained late one night to Helen, "I know he is right. Bobby and I agree, yet this is the same fellow that sat with the president and me as we literally begged him to work his magic on the Hill to pass civil rights, the housing bill, taxes, medical care. But nothing. He did nothing. Now it has all changed. Now he is determined to pass it as the president's legacy when the truth is, he and I know this will, in the end, become Johnson's legacy."

Helen tried to understand her husband's concerns as best she could. She tried desperately to understand his pain, heartache, and guilt over Jack's death. Yet she believed in Johnson and felt that not only did he need Kenny and the Kennedy men to stay, but Kenny needed to stay for himself. He needed a mission to keep his mind off the pain, but she was careful in how she presented this to him.

"I understand, Kenny," she said. "But he needs you. He

needs both you and Bobby. The country needs you. It is about not only John Kennedy's legacy, but about the country."

His plain-speaking sister Justine was more direct. "Look, you are the luckiest guy to be in a position where another president is asking for your help to run the country and his agenda. By saying yes, you ensure John Kennedy's agenda. It is not about you, for God's sake, it is about the country."

So it was that Johnson's first important move as president was to prevent even the appearance of an exodus, and to reinforce his still very tentative ties with the northern power blocs that made up John Kennedy's Democratic party. The new president felt he had been patient, understanding—maybe overly so. But he felt it was time for Kenny to "get his ass back to The White House and to work. I've a got a damn country to run. I need everybody."

Kenny, however, was still in emotional pain and not at all sure he belonged in Lyndon Johnson's White House.

CHAPTER NINE
EMANCIPATION

In those early months of the transition, Kenny realized that it would be but a matter of time before Johnson would have to make the presidency his own. It was not just Bobby and Kenny who were finding it difficult to adjust to the new president. Johnson's men had never held such positions of power in the fishbowl of Washington politics and they were finding the adjustment a difficult one to make. President Johnson himself was under enormous pressure in those early months to keep the Kennedy men happy and Kennedy's agenda on track while at the same time exerting his own presidential power without seeming to do so. Johnson was not a man of such careful exertions of power and occasionally his impatience to be his own man reared its head.

In those early days, a Kennedy intimate went to visit Johnson one night for dinner. He mentioned that just before his trip to Texas, Kennedy had planned to name two distinguished Harvard professors to appointments within the government. One was economist Seymour Harris, who was to be named ambassador to Uruguay. He also mentioned that Arthur Schlesinger had gotten

Kennedy's approval for Samuel Beer, another Harvard man, to be named to the Federal Reserve. The Kennedy friend explained that the appointment had been cleared just before Kennedy left for Texas. "Arthur Schlesinger feels he will be an excellent choice," he explained to the new president.

Johnson sipped his drink, then put it down with force. Leaning in close to his visitor, he replied, "Arthur Schlesinger isn't running Latin American policy anymore." In the end neither Harris nor Beer were named to any posts in Johnson's administration.

Kenny and Bobby came to understand this quickly. When a Kennedy friend came up for an appointment, something that Jack had already greenlighted, Kenny was quick to change the scenario to ensure success. He explained to the president that the fellow in question had been suggested by Speaker McCormack and since they needed his support for the civil rights bill . . . Kenny left the statement unfinished. The new president smiled and agreed.

"You may be putting one over on me, Kenny, but either way I don't want to upset the Speaker," Johnson said. The man was appointed, but increasingly those kinds of victories would be fewer and farther between. While Kenny retained the title he had under President Kennedy, he shared neither the history nor trust with Johnson that he had with Kennedy. In addition, Kenny's tight relationship with Bobby made him a source of constant suspicion for Johnson, who remained convinced that Bobby saw himself as the president in exile and was just waiting for his chance.

Kenny had no luck convincing the new president that Bobby was so wrapped up in his grief at the moment, he had hardly thought about the presidency.

Given events and the power of the memory of John Kennedy, it is perhaps understandable that Johnson felt at times threatened by Bobby's ambition and, indeed, by the ghost of John Kennedy himself. Johnson was in a situation where it had to appear that he was just the caretaker of Kennedy's legacy, while behind the scenes moving to take the levers of power for himself. But he could not be seen to be doing so. It would, he feared, look unseemly and disrespectful to the slain president's memory. But it was a difficult balancing act, one fraught with landmines.

For example, Kenny had gotten a call at a few days before Christmas from a distraught Pierre Salinger. Salinger, Kennedy's press secretary, was a good pal of Kenny and Bobby, having gotten his start during their tenure at the Rackets Committee. Kenny saw him as a bit of younger brother and was deeply protective of him. In fact, on more than one occasion Jack had been frustrated with Pierre's youthful enthusiasm in the press office. Several times he mentioned to Kenny the idea of bringing in someone with more previous White House experience to oversee the office. Kenny always balked and persuaded Jack against the idea.

"You can get more experience, but you cannot replace Pierre's loyalty to you," he said. "He will always have your back." Despite his misgivings, Jack relented. Pierre stayed in place. But it was this very loyalty that now was a problem for Salinger with the new president. Johnson had called Salinger and ordered him to convene a meeting at the White House of all the assistant secretaries for public affairs. For these loyal Kennedy men, all of whom had stayed in place when Kennedy died, their job was to shape the image of their departments and the administration in the public sector. Their job was to be the public face of their departments to the press corps.

The men waited uneasily for over half an hour for the new president. Though Salinger had convened the meeting at the president's order, it was apparent he had no idea why they were there. This only added to everyone's sense of unease. It was something that never would have happened under Kennedy. If such a meeting were called, Kenny would have made sure Pierre was armed with the reasons why. Instead he was left flat-footed in front of the men that supposedly reported to him.

When the president finally strode into the room, it was apparent by his expression and demeanor that, as Salinger said later, "he was clearly upset and out of sorts. I had no idea why." The men stood uncomfortably as the new president entered. There was no witty repartee as there might have been under Kennedy. Instead the new president demanded to know why, as he put it, "such high priced talent, whose exact job description eludes me . . . why you are not earning your pay?"

The men stood in stunned silence. Nobody knew quite what to say or to what he was referring. Johnson continued: "You are not getting my picture on the front page the way you did with President Kennedy. I want to know why. And, if you can't do it, then maybe this isn't the right place for you anymore."

Leaning forward, his face visibly angry, he said that that very day, the only front-page display featuring the president of the United States was a story about the annual lighting of the Christmas tree on the south lawn of the White House. "That's it! That's all you have done," he snarled. He then went on to make clear there was "a new sheriff in town." He explained that he planned to go to Texas and the ranch for Christmas. "I do not want any major news announcements in Washington while I am gone. Any request you have will be sent to me in Texas and they will be made there from the Texas White House." With that he rose and strode out, leaving Salinger and these men open-mouthed and in shock. John Kennedy had never bothered with such controls. He felt he had put good men in those posts and he trusted them to do their jobs. If they had a question or concern it went to Kenny. Kennedy never paid any attention to such matters.

As Kenny listened to Pierre tell this story, he tried gently to remind him that Johnson was not Kennedy. A new president would have his own style. Yet even as he said it, he felt his stomach tighten. This represented a raid on his personal power. Kenny was increasingly unsure whether he had the stomach for such turf battles. For his part, Pierre was much clearer: "I can't work like this, Kenny. And you tell Bobby I won't."

What was clear to Kenny, Pierre, and Bobby was that Johnson was moving to consolidate his power. As reporter Rowland Evans put it, by "lecturing the government's top public relations men on their jobs, Johnson was subtly enhancing his own power by driving the point home that these men were now under his personal scrutiny now and had better watch their step if they wanted to keep their jobs. He intended to make them Johnson men."

While it can be said the Kennedy men were treated with respect, it was evident from Kenny on down that they were having trouble adjusting to the new president's regime. Robert Novak noted at the time that "Kennedy had delegated work and decision-making. He felt he had chosen the right men for the jobs and could trust them. Johnson did not like to delegate anything." He wanted reports from his advisors in writing, and they had been accustomed to brief succinct verbal communications with Kennedy. O'Donnell could not recall the last time he had been asked for a memo in writing. He and Jack simply spoke. Kenny would give him his view and Kennedy would make a decision, which Kenny would then execute.

Johnson, on the other hand, had a habit of walking around and around a problem, analyzing it this way and that way, and seeking advice on how to deal with it from many different advisors, none of whom knew the identity of the others. Kennedy was direct, succinct, and loathed tons of paper and memos. His mind grasped a problem quickly and he had a tight inner circle with whom he would consult. The decisions were sent outward from there. Any debate or discussion was kept to that circle.

Kenny, like Pierre, found Johnson's style confusing and, at times, difficult to handle. The style also set up turf battles for the new president's ear with men who would never have gotten near Kennedy, which Kenny found deeply tiresome. Kenny also found himself, despite his position, on the outside looking in, often being told of decisions after the fact—something that would never have happened under Kennedy.

"There was not a decision my brother made," Bobby Kennedy would later explain of Kenny's role and power, "not one decision he made that he did not involve and consult Kenny on. They might not always agree, but my brother always involved him in the decision and Kenny was often the very last person my brother talked to when making that decision."

That was extraordinary power. Yet with Johnson, despite the kind words, Kenny was on the outside. His powerful and longstanding relationship with Jack Kennedy, and his deep brotherly friendship with Bobby, continued to make him suspect to Johnson and his men.

There was no greater evidence of the changing of the guard than when the Johnson White House pulled up stakes and went to Texas for Christmas, leaving Kenny and Pierre behind. In all the years Kenny had been with Jack, wherever he went, Kenny had been there. This time, to his great relief, he was to admit to Pierre that he had been left behind. As he and Pierre shared drinks and memories at Duke Zeibert's one evening after Johnson had left town, Pierre said the obvious to Kenny: "We can't last long here. We cannot."

They sat in silence nursing their drinks and their memories of better days. "No," Kenny agreed, still looking straight ahead, "but we stay until Bobby says otherwise."

"You have to understand," Kenny explained later to journalist and friend Sander Vanocur. "Johnson had known Bobby and I since 1955 or so. He had then been the powerful majority leader and he saw us as he should have, as two young kids still wet behind the ears when it came to national politics. He and Bobby just never hit it off and as these things tend to do, the more powerful Bobby became the less Johnson liked him. Bobby just seemed incapable of showing the necessary political deference that Johnson's ego required. The situation was only worsened by the disaster in Los Angeles over the vice presidency in 1960. They never recovered."

As vice president, Kenny continued, Johnson "saw conspiracy everywhere when it came to his relationship with Bobby Kennedy. Johnson had all these theories about Bobby being out to get him, replace him on the ticket in '64, and then after he became president this only got worse." It included things such as the scandal involving Bobby Baker, Johnson's right hand that Justice was investigating, but the story had been first investigated by journalist Clark Mollenhoff and brought by him to Bobby at Justice.

The truth was Bobby Kennedy had nothing to do with it. That is my point. It broke upon Bobby Kennedy as it broke upon us. He may have had his private feelings about it, about Johnson and Bobby Baker, I know he did, but you know Bobby was always the ultimate professional. Bobby would never do anything that would potentially hurt his brother, ever. There were some stories that we heard floating around the town that Bobby Baker and Bobby Kennedy had a dislike for each other going back to the campaign, because Bobby Kennedy was the president's campaign manager and Bobby Baker had been Johnson's.

There had been a clash between them. That was simply not true. Bobby Kennedy never even met Bobby Baker until after the convention in 1960 and even that was by accident. I had never met Bobby Baker in my life. Bobby and I had been in the Senate together and never ever did we deal with Bobby Baker.

There just isn't any question that Lyndon Johnson was going to be nominated by the Democratic Party if Jack Kennedy had his way. He put it on the record at a press conference and he would not back off of that. He was as cold as ice about it. It was a cold, hard fact that politically there was no place for the president to go on this issue. Now whether or not Bobby Kennedy or some his entourage really understood the problem, I would say they did not. From Bobby and his entourage's point of view the real problem with Lyndon Johnson was not 1964, but Lyndon Johnson as the Democratic nominee in 1968. That is a different problem than the one the president was wrestling with as he faced the '64 election. The leaks that did occur from the Department of Justice and might have occurred from some of Bobby's friends in detrimental to the vice president would serve no purpose. John Kennedy, being a very pragmatic politician, had picked Lyndon Johnson over the objections of many people, because he thought he would help him get elected president. He realized what the real role of the vice president involved. John Kennedy would pick him again for the very same reasons.

Quite simply, a clash between the Southerners and the Northerners at a convention would cause further deterioration of whatever opposition might be in 1964. Therefore, it was never contemplated by the president of the United

States and therefore never entered our political counsels that Lyndon Johnson not be a candidate for vice president in 1964.

Now what would occur in '68 was four years away. There was, or so it seemed, plenty of time. What the president (Kennedy) thought about it—he did think about it—but what he thought about it politically I do not think anyone knows and nobody will ever know. We discussed it at great length and he never, ever talked about getting rid of Johnson.

We must remember the circumstances. John Kennedy was never a fellow to look four or five years ahead of time. He knew all too well . . . how fleeting life can be. History will foretell rightly that John Kennedy was right to choose Johnson, even given the circumstances. I am not sure what other man, given what happened, could have brought the country together again so quickly after that weekend. John Kennedy knew what he was doing when he selected Johnson, on a number of levels.

The president and I did discuss, at times, the larger issues down the road as they figured into 1968. We discussed that there would be great complications in 1968. That he would be placed in a most difficult position in which he would have to select a successor who, logically, should be Lyndon Johnson. Obviously, his personal preference would have been his brother Bobby. However, he knew that would very difficult to choose Bobby in 1968 unless, as he put it, in the next four years Bobby were to grow at a startling rate. He understood that the dynasty thing would be a great problem, but I do not think he thought much beyond that. I do know how much he thought about whether or not Lyndon could measure up the problems or not. He had had some concerns about that in his personal experience with Johnson, but he was hopeful that would improve.

Kennedy's main concern with Johnson was personal experience and his difficulty in getting Johnson to take a more active role as vice president. He had a tremendously difficult time getting him to make a decision. He had trouble even getting him to involve himself with Congress, where the president had originally thought Johnson would really enjoy himself. "I know that aspect concerned him—the thought of Johnson running on his own in 1968. He was concerned that Johnson would not be an activist president and that disturbed him to a degree," Kenny remembered.

"President Kennedy was disturbed that Johnson did not take a more activist role and did not and would not go on the record for many of the crucial decisions," Bobby said. "The president certainly hoped that in a second term that he would involve himself on the record in more decisions than he did."

According to Kenny, Kennedy's "theory on why he, Johnson, didn't [take a more active role] was that—and this is my own feeling and the president's feeling—that he felt a senator, like Johnson, who was nurtured in the Senate and lived in the Senate, had a great difficulty to make a decision. In the Senate, they want to discuss things, they want to make speeches, but they do not want to ever really get down and make the tough decisions."

President Kennedy pointed out to Kenny "that senators can take any and all sides of an issue, because they do not have to make that final decision. For example, what we do in Berlin about the [Berlin] Wall, well, it is the president who makes the final call on whether we do or do not do something."

Kenny:

President Kennedy felt that the vice president had so much

of this sort of thinking in his system that he simply could not make a decisive statement on a situation. Johnson liked to weigh all sides of an issue and often would, arguing all sides of particular issue. The president would have these meetings and Johnson would weight all sides and the president would say, with some frustration, "But what do you think?"

Well, John Kennedy did give him the benefit of the doubt at the beginning. As events continued, he became a little concerned. . . . President Kennedy felt he, Johnson, needed to participate more. He was sympathetic to the situation, and I know I have said this before, that the president explained to me what he felt Lyndon's position was vis-à-vis Ken O'Donnell, for example. John Kennedy warned me that, you know, Lyndon felt strange that he had to call me, Ken O'Donnell, whom he once knew as a former clerk in the Senate, and now he had to call me if he wanted to meet with the president.

Lyndon was a very proud man and this was a difficult thing for him to do and we were all to bend over backward to appreciate Lyndon's problem and be respectful of his problem. For example, at one point, all you heard was the stories being leaked to the press from the White House about stories that were critical of the vice president. President Kennedy was furious; he wanted to find the source of the leak and have the person or persons fired, no matter who they were. He was furious because the president felt such stories were hurtful to Lyndon Johnson, his family, and, quite frankly, hurtful to him as the president, as well.

"He has no choice, he has to make the presidency his own," Kenny said to Bobby over lunch at their favorite haunt, Duke Zeibert's, a restaurant much loved by the political powers that be in Washington. The place was owned by Jewish immigrant Duke Zeibert, who had become a good friend to Kenny as the place was just walking distance from the White House. The walls were covered with photos from the Kennedy years. With its deep red leather booths, the place provided some privacy and was a special favorite and haven of sorts for Kenny and Bobby—Jack's "Irish Mafia" in exile.

"Why?" Bobby asked, his voice soft, still heavy with grief. He swirled his milk around in his glass as he spoke. For his part, Kenny downed a beer, teasing Bobby for being such a heavy hitter. Bobby smiled sadly.

"Look, Bobby, your brother did the same thing. Each president must make it their own," Kenny explained, though he knew Bobby already knew that.

Bobby heaved a heavy sigh. "Yeah, I guess. So why are we still here?"

"You know why," Kenny answered, nodding a thank you as the white-gloved waiter brought him another beer and Bobby another milk.

"Remind me," Bobby said, as he stared almost blankly at his glass of milk, almost as if the glass itself held the answers to his pain.

"Because it is your brother's agenda—civil rights, the tax cut among other things," Kenny said. Kenny's coal-black eyes were watching Bobby closely. Bobby sat up and leaned back.

"Yeah, I know. That stuff has been bottled up in Congress. How the hell is going to get it through? His track record was pretty unimpressive so far. I mean, Jack wasn't too happy. You know that. What's changed?"

Kenny nodded. "I agree, but he wasn't president then."

The words hung in the air between them. They said little for a long time, their food largely untouched between them. Just then Duke brought the telephone over to the table. Putting his hand over the receiver, he whispered, "It is the president for you, Kenny."

Kenny shuddered for a moment and picked up the phone, listening as the operator brought on the president. The Texas drawl and loud voice cut through the air. Bobby could hear him plainly. Bobby shook his head, indicating he would rather not have Lyndon know he was there, but of course that was not Kenny's style.

"I still cannot get used to it," Kenny mouthed to Bobby as he informed the president he was sitting with the attorney general, lest Johnson say something that pissed Bobby off. Kenny was determined to see Jack's agenda, at least civil rights, through, and help Johnson and other Democrats win in 1964 before he left. To do that successfully he, Larry O'Brien, and the other Kennedy men knew they needed to keep Bobby and Lyndon on the same page and getting along, at least for the moment. Although only back for a short time, Kenny was beginning to see the balancing act would not work for long and that such a political tightrope might require someone more adept than Kenny.

"Mr. President, I am sitting with the attorney general, I thought you should know." After a momentary pause where Lyndon had to take a moment, he seemed pleased.

"Good, Kenny," he drawled, "That's real good. I need to talk to you both about this civil rights bill. I was gonna ask you to call the attorney general. Can you both come up now?"

Bobby sat stone faced as Kenny replied for him. "Yes, Mr. President. Absolutely."

"Good," Lyndon replied, hanging up abruptly.

Kenny shook his head and laughed, replacing the receiver in the cradle. "Well, so much for him trusting me," Kenny said. "Day two of being back and I am having lunch with you."

Bobby chuckled as they slid out of the booth. "If I am going to be miserable, you might as well be miserable with me."

"Thanks," Kenny replied, patting Bobby on the shoulder as they headed for the door. "You've always been a pal."

The laughter was momentary. As they hit Connecticut Avenue and turned right to walk towards the White House, the magnitude of their loss seemed to suck all the oxygen out of the air. They walked in silence most of the rest of the way. Occasionally passersby would recognize Bobby, but the pain etched on his face seemed to keep them at a safe distance.

Just as they approached the gate, Bobby stopped and took a deep breath. "By the way, I have not come back to work yet. How did he know I'd be with you?"

Kenny laughed. "Where else would Kennedy's government-in-exile be except at a bar?"

Bobby shrugged and laughed softly. Sure, it was gallows humor, but these days they had to find what levity they could, where they could.

But here they sat talking about Jack's stalled civil rights bill with a man who Bobby simply didn't trust or feel comfortable with. Bobby sat wordless as Johnson outlined his plans to break the impasse. He seemed uncomfortable in his brother's old office and sat on the edge of the seat, as if preparing to jump up and run at any moment. Lyndon seemed almost oblivious to Bobby's discomfort. Kenny, in his customary spot leaning against the wall, thought that Bobby physically winced each time the president said, "We must do it for him." Kenny said little, but finally he could stand it no more and suggested that Bobby had better not keep Ethel waiting.

Of course, Kenny didn't know where Ethel was at the moment, but he felt the situation was too uncomfortable to continue. Bobby gave the president a distant handshake and Kenny offered to walk him out. When they finally reached the gate, Kenny asked him what he thought. Bobby shrugged. He stared straight ahead for while. "I will stay on just long enough to get the bill through. You?" he asked Kenny.

Kenny shrugged. "I agree, but I want to see he gets reelected by a strong margin. I want to help Larry, Walter [Jenkins], Moyers, and Valenti get up to speed. Then I think we will all go."

Bobby nodded. "Agreed," was all he said. Squeezing Kenny's shoulder, Bobby nodded again and said, "I guess we both have to figure out what's next, but we cannot stay here."

"Yeah." Kenny nodded. "He deserves his own team. Every president does."

"Do you think he'll break the legislative logjam?" Bobby asked again.

Kenny shrugged. "I hope so. His presidency may depend on it."

Bobby nodded again in reply. "Yeah, I guess. More important to me is Jack's legacy."

"He knows that, Bobby," Kenny said quietly.

Bobby smiled and punched Kenny's arm. "Keep me posted," he said as he began to walk towards the Lincoln Memorial.

"Bobby," Kenny said, "I'll keep you posted for as long as he keeps me around. And by the way, the Justice Department is that way." Kenny pointed in the opposite direction of where Bobby was headed. "Your car is that way."

Bobby shook his head. "I am going up to Arlington and visit Jack's grave." Bobby began to walk, his head down, shoulders stooped by the weight of his grief, hands stuffed in his pockets and wearing only a suit coat despite the cold.

Kenny watched him walk away with his hands stuffed in his pockets. His head was down and he was lost in thought. He was a sad figure as he headed towards Arlington and his brother's grave. Kenny stood for a moment watching him. Then, having reached his decision, he looked back towards the White House.

He thought, "Oh hell, he doesn't need me."

Then Kenny did something unthinkable before now. It was something he would never have dreamed of if Jack were still president. He turned back towards Bobby's retreating figure and trotted quickly to catch up with him. Bobby looked up at Kenny. "Won't he be mad at you?"

Kenny shrugged. "No, he understands. Besides, I don't give a damn anyway." They continued in silence for another block.

"Thanks," Bobby said. Kenny nodded.

"Always got your back. Somebody has to keep you out of trouble. It's not so easy, you know."

Bobby laughed softly. "Well, you are probably not the right fellow for that assignment."

The friends laughed and continued their sad silent walk to Arlington.

Back at the White House, the whirl of action had not stopped. The new president was too busy working the phones to Congress to notice that Kenny had not returned.

CHAPTER TEN
THE JOHNSON STYLE

While John Kennedy's stricken family and his men in and out of government waded through the sadness of the first Christmas without their president, the Johnson family had Christmas at the western White House—Johnson's ranch in Texas. For them it was an equally challenging holiday, but for different reasons. Once there at his beloved ranch, Lyndon began to realize the time had come to finalize the transition from the Kennedy years to what would be the Johnson years. Exactly how this change would occur was slowly beginning to take shape in the new president's mind. Perhaps at some level, Kenny and Bobby even understood this was politically necessary for the party, as well as the nation, but, as Kenny said to his wife one evening, "it doesn't make it any damn easier to accept."

Down in Texas, Lyndon Johnson saw this "Christmas week as the beginning of the end of his transition as president." There remained only the president's address to the opening of the second session of the 88th Congress on January 8, 1964.

Upon his return to Washington, Johnson called a meeting of his foreign advisors for one final discussion of his State of the Union message. "There was gathered there," Bob Novak recalled, "three layers of advisors, each separate from the other, each with its uncommon tradition but all now joined together. The first layer was the Kennedy-holdovers: Rusk and McNamara, the CIA's John McCone, McGeorge Bundy, Arthur Schlesinger, and Walt Rostow of the State Department policy staff, Don Wilson of USI; the second layer was the core of Johnson's new insiders: Moyers, Valenti, and of course Walter Jenkins; finally the third layer: the triumvirate of Fortas, Clifford, and Rowe. One common purpose united this diverse group—to help Lyndon Johnson succeed."

Johnson stood and took the floor. No longer showing any hint of uneasiness or hesitation, he had now, just as Kennedy had before him, taken on the "mantle of the presidency." "Remember," he cautioned, "I still talk two and half times as slow as Kennedy. Keep it short. I want you to understand my thinking as you write this draft. John Kennedy had left this nation in excellent military condition, so we can just make that clear."

Then, according to those present, Johnson launched into a highly subjective discussion about peace. "I don't want to get into a position," he explained, "where at breakfast I get a new message from Khrushchev saying how much *he* is for peace when all I read from the United States is how we are strong enough to blow up the world." This, Johnson explained to those present, was the tone he wanted to establish with his speech.

He then moved to foreign aid and explained further: Foreign aid was always a problem, but it could not be fought out on a basis of "it helps our national security," but rather seeing it as an "obligation of the richer nations to help the poorer nations." He then moved swiftly through his domestic agenda: "housing, urban affairs, and my brand new poverty program." He asked about the word "poverty." It worried him. It might send the wrong signal to Congress. Was there a better word? Nobody had any answers. Many admitted later to being taken aback by the sheer breadth of Johnson's legislative knowledge, his agenda and ambitions, especially the Kennedy holdovers, who had seen everything Kennedy had fought for the most part bottled up by Congress. How exactly did Johnson propose to get all this moved through Congress?

"I hate the word poverty," Johnson explained as he went through a long, winding monologue outlining his Texas-sized ambitions for his domestic agenda. Those gathered were amazed at his complete mastering of all the details, which, given his role as majority leader, should not have been surprising. But the Kennedy men in particular were struck by how completely different this Lyndon Johnson sounded than the man they had experienced when he was Kennedy's vice president.

"But it's not about poverty," Johnson insisted emotionally when trying to describe the importance of his social agenda. "It's wastage of resources and human lives. It is just unfair. We can do better for our people. We will do better."

As Johnson prepared for his first major speech to Congress as president, those around him noticed a shift. One aide reported to Kenny anonymously how, as the sadness around the death of John Kennedy began to fade somewhat, Johnson began to revert to his more natural instincts. The living room at the ranch became a sort of grand central station with aides shuffling in and out as the new president began to assert his priorities. Though neither Kenny or Bobby were there, they began to hear reports that the old imperious Johnsonian style from his Senate years began to emerge even in the handling of the Kennedy echelon and holdovers. "In some ways," Kenny said, "his natural temperament and political style had been held in check during the Kennedy years. It was somewhat inevitable that now, standing on his own, he would revert to his own approach. It was not the kind of approach that would have enamored him to John Kennedy."

According to those present, the monologues during these meetings went on and on; the meetings went far into the night. The gathered groups would finally leave in the early hours of the next day, exhausted and drained. But there was one thing that everyone who left that meeting completely understood—who was in charge.

"In six weeks since the murder of Jack Kennedy, Lyndon Johnson had pulled into his own hands all the threads of the United States government. The presidency was his, the transition was over. The bitter memory of Dallas was still overpowering, but the new president had achieved his first imperative. There was confidence in the land again," reported Rowland Evans and Bob Novak in one of their regular columns.

As Johnson saw it, the time was now to get started. And as he explained, "the first step is taming Congress."

"For thirty-two years, Capitol Hill has been my home . . . We have a unique opportunity and obligation to prove the success of our system, to disprove those cynics and critics at home and abroad who question our purpose and competence."

With this simple statement, Lyndon Johnson became the president in full measure. The transition was over. John F. Kennedy was now gone and Lyndon Johnson had finally declared his independence and taken over the levers of political power that was the presidency of the United States.

The Johnson approach would prove to be far different and more successful than Kennedy could have imagined when Johnson was brought on as vice president. Johnson exerted a charm. He was persuasive when necessary. He could bully as called for. And he was determined to push his legislative agenda. Given Kennedy's frustration with Johnson as vice president when it came to Capitol Hill, Jack would likely have been thunderstruck to have watched Johnson in action. Kenny later recalled:

> The president had been thoroughly frustrated with the performance of Johnson as vice president. He had simply refused to use his considerable leverage to move the president's legislative agenda forward, claiming he was incapable of doing so. He treated John Kennedy's legislative priorities as if they were not his own. To watch him now was amazing and somewhat frustrating personally for me at times. Why hadn't he done this before now? We did not want to be seen as not being supportive, but still this newfound self-confidence was puzzling to us. Where had this fellow been when President Kennedy tried to get him to intervene with Congress?

The truth was that, as Sander Vanocur noted, "Lyndon Johnson's relationship with Congress and individual members was closer than any time in recent memory. After all, just as he had said in his speech, this had been his political home for thirty-four years until 1960." The truth was also a bit different than Kenny and Bobby might have wanted to admit in the wake of Jack's death. Evans and Novak noted in a column at the time that Kennedy, unlike Johnson, did not have a great deal of deep relationships on Capitol Hill. In fact, "senior ranking Democrats who had seen President Kennedy only on official business or social events had easy and casual access to President Johnson. The informal tone of the White House under Lyndon and Lady Bird Johnson was more congenial to middle-aged legislators of the South and West than the high, dashing style of the Kennedys."

"This change in relations," they continued, "between Capitol Hill and the White House was inevitable with Lyndon Johnson as president, no matter what the prevailing problems." After all, Capitol Hill was Johnson's political home. In the first weeks of his presidency, his attention would naturally return there, to his comfort zone. While presidents rarely enjoy traveling the seventeen blocks from the White House to Capitol Hill and Kennedy surely did not, Lyndon Johnson still thought of the Hill as his home. Kenny noted to his wife Helen, "I think he finds solace in returning there while he gets the role of the presidency under control."

His constant trips reflected his "love of the place," the president told Kenny. He traveled back and forth to the White House in those early days, said Bob Novak, as if his "very life depended upon it." In some ways, perhaps it did. For example, without advance warning, during his first week in office he dropped in on the weekly luncheon of the Texas delegation, startling its members, who rarely were treated to a visit from a president and certainly had never once seen Kennedy. But for Lyndon, this was his regular stop when he had been in Congress and as vice president.

John McCormack later told Kenny that the following day, the new president had arrived in his office for a "surprise visit" and stayed so long he joined them for an afternoon drink with House members in his old office where he used to sit as a member of Sam Rayburn's so-called Board of Education. The Board of Education were members that regularly met with Rayburn, the legislative master. They would meet for drinks to discuss legislation, map strategy, and swap stories. Lyndon had been a regular member, attending faithfully. But it wasn't just that Johnson was visiting Congress; he was constantly inviting members to join him in his home at the Elms while he waited a respectful time for Jackie Kennedy to pack, make arrangements, and move into her new home in Averill Harriman's house in Georgetown. Once moved into the White House, Lyndon's invitations to members only increased. He would invite them for luncheon, drinks, and dinners organized by Lady Bird at the spur of the moment. He seemed to thrive on, and need, the company. It was truly an open door policy, which was far different than when Jack and Jackie Kennedy had been there.

Evans and Novak noted at the time: "In the early weeks of the Johnson presidency and, in fact, right up until the 1964 election, relations between the president and individual members of Congress were closer than they had been in recent memory. Senior Democrats who had seen President Kennedy only on official business or at social events had easy and casual access to President Johnson."

The difference in the two styles reflected the personality of the men in the Oval Office. Where Jack Kennedy had urged Kenny to keep the members of Congress at arm's length unless there was a specific reason for a meeting, Johnson wanted them up all the time, often going around staff, including Kenny. "He would pick up the phone and call them himself, invite them up for lunch or dinner or after dinner drinks. Often I did not know about it until they walked through the door," Kenny said.

"I cannot do my job this way," Kenny told Bobby. Kenny had been much more than a gatekeeper for Jack Kennedy. They had a relationship that Kenny described as "one in a million." The trust was complete. He had been the one who helped craft Jack's climb to the White House.

"Kenny was more chief of staff than anything else. He was the gatekeeper," Bobby said. "There wasn't a decision the president [Kennedy] made that Kenny was not involved with. That was true from the beginning. Lyndon went around him constantly. It undermined his position, so understandably, as his job and influence were reduced he spent less and less time there."

In truth, unlike Jack Kennedy, who lived a highly compartmentalized life, Lyndon Johnson had never had a social life distinct from his political life. The two were inextricably blended.

This change in the relationship between the White House and Congress was "deeply underscored by the fact that in the late autumn 1963, before Kennedy's death, Congress was widely regarded as the number one problem for the White House," Kenny said.

In truth, Larry O'Brien admitted,

> Johnson inherited from Kennedy what seemed on the surface the worst Congressional revolt since the days of Harry Truman, resulting in an atrophy of the New Frontier's legislative dreams. President Kennedy was frustrated with Congress and their inaction. It seems understandable he would expect the former Majority Leader, Lyndon Johnson, to help break the deadlock. What I think President Kennedy failed to consider was that once Johnson was removed as majority leader and not given any real power as vice president, his ability to master an unruly Congress was severely limited.

Larry O'Brien, Kennedy's congressional aide, who would stay on with Johnson, marking the final disillusion of Jack Kennedy's "Irish Mafia," noted later that he could wring nothing out of Congress when Kennedy was in the White House. "When Johnson came in," he said, "the phone calls began to get returned, meetings were no longer postponed indefinitely, and mark-up hearings on the president's agenda began in earnest."

As is always the case in Washington, whispers began to

surface, first among some New Frontiersmen who stayed on with Johnson, that the Kennedy legislative record was a "weak spot on his presidency." While Kennedy's place in history would be assured by his brilliance during the thirteen days of the Cuban missile crisis, his failure to move any legislation through successfully or break the congressional deadlock loomed over his record. All this talk infuriated Bobby and Kenny. "None of them had the guts to say it to his face when he was alive," Bobby said to Kenny angrily. "And none of them ever offered an alternative strategy to his approach."

While Kenny agreed, he also reminded Bobby what Jack had told them one evening during the missile crisis: "If we make the wrong call, all these fellows will be the first to say, 'I told you so' and if we make the right decision, then they will all claim it was their idea." Kenny also reminded Bobby, and himself, that as hurtful as they found these remarks, Jack had been a political realist. He would no doubt be pleased that his agenda was being passed and that Johnson had embraced it entirely. Indeed, he was pushing hard to make it successful. "If things were going to happen this way," Kenny said, "I think your brother would be more focused on getting his agenda passed than worrying about his place in history."

Bobby said little in return. They knew that was the truth, but both men would have given anything to have Jack back, legislative success or no. But that wasn't to be, and both were now having to adjust to a new era and new president. It was the Johnson era—soon to be dubbed the "Great Society"—and for Bobby and Kenny, the New Frontier was increasingly in the rearview mirror.

CHAPTER ELEVEN

"I'VE GOT ME A BOBBY PROBLEM"

"It was during that gloomy Christmas season that many of us Kennedy Frontiersmen, as the press had dubbed us, wondered if we could stay on working for any other president than President Kennedy," Kenny recalled.

It took Kenny well over a month to return to work. In the end, he did so only with the urging of his wife, Bobby, and President Johnson. Dave Powers had already gone back to work part-time, telling Kenny, "I just couldn't sit around the house and think anymore."

Later, over drinks, Dave told Kenny he had been in the White House one day attending a reception with Johnson's chief presidential aide, Bill Moyers, and Walter Jenkins. They were waiting for the new president to join them and then they would go with him to the reception. As the president emerged from the Oval Office with Lady Bird, Johnson looked over at Kenny's empty desk. "That's Kenny O'Donnell's desk. I don't want anyone sitting at it or using it. Hear?"

The Irish wake for President Kennedy went on for well over a month and straight through the Christmas season. "I went to Palm Beach during the Christmas season and had several long talks there with Jackie and other Kennedy family members about whether to return to the White House full-time or not. The two people whose opinions most concerned me were Jackie and Bobby. One night after dinner Jackie and I were reminiscing about President Kennedy and she took a moment to tell me that she did not feel strongly one way or the other about it."

"Kenny," she said, "whatever you decide to do is all right with me. I think if you can help him to get Jack's agenda passed that would be good. But I think for all of us right now, the next steps are unclear and sure to be temporary ones."

The visit also provided for some long walks and talks with Bobby as they both wrestled with their grief and guilt over Jack's murder.

Bobby was deeply troubled that perhaps his aggressive posture towards the mafia had come back to haunt them. I worried that my decision to make some changes to the trip had made him vulnerable. I told Bobby my job had been to keep him safe. I had failed. We both worried about Cuba. In the end, we decided to eventually conduct a private investigation of our own to get some answers.

Bobby and I agreed that if Kennedy's key people left the White House in droves that it might cause a split in the Democratic ranks during the coming presidential election campaign. At least, we thought, we owed it to President Kennedy to do our best to keep Senator Barry Goldwater out of office.

Bobby completely agreed. He also pointed out that a walkout of Kennedy aides might give the totally wrong impression that we were blaming Johnson for President Kennedy's death in Texas. Bobby explained his thinking this way: "I think such an impression could not only cost Johnson the election in '64, but could do permanent political damage to the Democratic Party. By staying I think we make it clear that we hold no grudges against either Johnson or Texas. I feel that is the least we owe my brother."

So with all those thoughts swirling in his mind and some added pressure from his wife and from Bobby, Kenny finally returned to work. But Kenny made it clear to Bobby, Helen, and most importantly President Johnson that he would only stay until after Johnson was safely reelected.

"I will stay until after the November election and that is it," he told President Johnson over a drink in the White House shortly after he returned from Palm Beach. While Johnson quickly agreed, he told aides he paid it "no mind." "In the end," he said, "we will make them into Johnson men. Kenny will become one of us."

While President Johnson was always careful and respectful of the Kennedy people, by the end of his State of the Union speech, he began to get restless. As best he could, he was determined to push the country forward and beyond mourning their slain president. He needed to start crafting his own agenda apart from Kennedy's, but he had to proceed with caution. To do that successfully meant getting the Kennedy men "back in the saddle."

"Hell, it's hard for all of us, but we got a country to run," he told Kenny with some frustration. "I am not immune from it, but I've got a job to do for this country."

Certainly nobody understood that better than Kenny and Bobby, but they still found it a bitter pill to swallow. "He simply wasn't John Kennedy," Kenny's sister, Justine, lamented later.

Her statement reflected the views of many of the Kennedy people still in the Johnson White House and nobody understood that more than Johnson himself.

The discussion of Bobby as a potential vice-presidential candidate really began back on December 11, 1963. As Kenny remembered it, he and his wife Helen had been invited by President Johnson to travel with the president and Mrs. Johnson on Air Force One to attend the funeral of Congressman William J. Green in Philadelphia. Green had been an important ally of President Kennedy. Johnson's political instincts had told him he would be wise to attend the funeral, draped, as it were, in the Kennedy aura. He understood attending the funeral with Kenny and Helen would send a signal to the political ranks within the Democratic Party that the Johnson and Kennedy people were still one. "Kennedy may not be in the picture anymore," Johnson told Kenny, "but we need to keep him in the frame."

Congressman Bill Green had been one of Kenny's dear friends. Kenny understood Johnson's political calculations in asking to attend with him and Helen, but he also knew how deeply appreciative both the family and the Democratic Party regulars in Philadelphia would be.

"No matter what differences, having a president of the United States attend is an important gesture for the family and the party. Bill Green would have loved it," Kenny said later to Bobby.

Kenny, recalling the event, said:

Along with everybody else who talked with Johnson at that time, I was bewildered by his later assertions in his memoirs some years later that he had no intention of running for the presidency in 1964 until Lady Bird persuaded him to seek the nomination on the day after the opening of the

Democratic convention, August 25, at Atlantic City. On the day we travelled to Bill Green's funeral, two weeks before the previous Christmas, Lyndon talked constantly about his plan to run for president in the coming year, and he continued to talk about it daily during the winter, spring, and summer of 1964 while I was working with him at the White House. When we were flying to Philadelphia on that cold December day he told me that he did not want Bobby Kennedy as his vice-presidential candidate: "Kenny," he said, "I don't want history to say I was elected to this office because I had Bobby on the ticket with me. But I'll take him if I need him."

Kenny grimaced when Johnson said this, though from a strictly political point of view he understood it. "In other words," Kenny said, "Lyndon was saying if the Republicans nominated a more liberal candidate than Barry Goldwater, Johnson would see himself as forced to take Bobby as his vice president to win support from labor and from Kennedy Democrats."

In fact, Kenny pointed out, "If the second Mrs. Nelson Rockefeller had not happened to give birth to Nelson A. Rockefeller Jr., only a few days before the California primary in 1964, the Democratic party might have had a Johnson-Bobby Kennedy ticket that fall."

Johnson made it clear to Kenny several times over the coming weeks, that if the Republicans nominated a more liberal candidate such as Rockefeller, Michigan governor George Romney, or Pennsylvania's William Scranton, he would have been forced to offer the vice presidency to Bobby in order to win.

"I don't like him too much, Kenny," Johnson said of Bobby, "and he doesn't like me too much either, I'll say that. But I'll take him if I've got no choice."

Kenny later pointed out, "Whether Bobby would have

accepted the offer is another highly doubtful question. During the six months after his brother's death, he was confused and uncertain about his future plans. He remarked to me one day over lunch at Sans Souci in Washington that his brother Teddy, then the senator from Massachusetts, thought the vice presidency was unworthy of his consideration."

But Bobby was understandably skeptical, given their history, about his ability to get along with Johnson. Kenny said, "The truth was, with Johnson delaying his choice of a running mate until it was safe enough to bypass Bobby, I decided, with strong encouragement from the Kennedy staff people and my friends in the labor movement, to promote Hubert Humphrey for the second place on the Democratic ticket in 1964. All of us in the Kennedy camp—Bobby, John Bailey, Larry O'Brien, Dick Daley, Jesse Unruh—admired Humphrey as a hardline liberal fighter for civil rights."

This was all fine, but Johnson did not want Humphrey on the ticket any more than he wanted Bobby. "The reasons were clear," Kenny said. "Johnson did not want to share the credit for his election with a vice-presidential nominee like Bobby or Humphrey, who had strong personal support from labor, the Negroes, the Jewish liberals and the Midwest farmers."

Bobby and Kenny guessed that Johnson's strategy was, as Kenny explained, "that if Goldwater was the nominee, he could win the nomination entirely on his own with some nonentity as the vice-presidential candidate. The truth was that Johnson would have been happiest if he could have campaigned alone that year without any vice-presidential candidate."

In Kenny's opinion, "If Bobby was out, as we expected him to be, then my job was to position Humphrey in such a way that Johnson had no choice but to take him. I felt we had enough leverage over Johnson to force him to accept a vice-presidential candidate of our choice, namely Hubert Humphrey, if Bobby did not want the nomination for himself. Johnson badly needed me and other Kennedy campaign veterans to promote his candidacy with Democratic leaders in various states and big Democratic cities throughout the country."

It was Kenny and Bobby's calculation that Johnson's own contacts within these vital Democratic strongholds was limited. His own political experience was limited to Texas and the Senate. During the Kennedy presidential campaign, Vice President Johnson had taken little notice of and participated very little in the inner workings of the Kennedy organization. This put Kenny and Bobby in a particular position of strength with regard to Johnson.

Kenny explained: "Bobby and I understood that he realized he could not win without us, so if Bobby is out as either the vice-presidential choice or the nominee, then Johnson must rely on us as he selects his vice-presidential pick. We knew if we played the game right, we could force our choice upon him and that was our plan."

"He might resist it," Bobby said later to Kenny, "but in the end he will have to take our choice and live with it."

The Kennedy people—specifically Kenny and Bobby—understood that Johnson was most eager to avoid a public fight with, as Johnson put it, "Bobby Kennedy or any of Bobby Kennedy's friends."

Kenny said Johnson was "obsessed that spring that Bobby might force himself onto the vice presidency, or maybe even make a bid for the presidency, by suddenly appearing at the convention and instigating a floor fight. Johnson asked me almost every day while I was at the White House if I knew what Bobby was planning."

"Why doesn't he withdraw and save all of us a lot of worry and trouble?" Johnson would ask. Kenny would shrug and explain to him that he, Kenny, "was getting lots of calls from party leaders across the country who were saying that Bobby would win a floor fight. They were calling and urging me to push Bobby to run."

The reality was that Kenny and Bobby were playing a bit of what Kenny called a "political cat and mouse game" with Johnson. Kenny admitted that he was "in a unique position":

In addition to my role in the White House, Johnson had made me executive director of his political campaign and at the same time I was the only communication contact he had with Bobby. Bobby would only speak to Johnson through me. While Bobby was still in the cabinet and as Attorney General, he and Johnson rarely spoke to each other. At events in which they both had to attend, both men worked hard to avoid having to interact and speak to each other.

This all worked to our advantage as we tried to leverage a situation which would force Johnson to accept Humphrey as the nominee for vice president.

When either man wanted the other man to know something, I was asked to pass along the message. Johnson knew I was being honest and straightforward in my dealings with him. He also knew that Bobby was one of my closest friends, and I had made it plain to Johnson that if Bobby decided to run for the vice presidency, I would resign from the White House staff to work for him.

Johnson understood and accepted Kenny's position, but it did make him suspect in some ways.

"I always felt that while Kenny was always straightforward with me, I knew Bobby was his priority," Johnson said later. "Naturally, that factored into our situation."

With that in mind, Johnson, not unskilled at political cat and mouse games himself, decided to, as Kenny put it, "diminish Bobby's image by seeking out another member of the Kennedy family for the vice presidency."

He called in a surprised Kennedy brother-in-law, head of the Peace Corps Sargent Shriver, to a meeting in the Oval Office. He offered him the vice presidency and suggested that two terms in the position would put him in the right place to run for the presidency himself in 1972. Kenny remembered hearing about this for the first time:

> I was sitting alone with [Johnson] in the Oval Office one day in March when the voice of Johnson aide Bill Moyers came on his interoffice talk box. Apparently not knowing that I was listening, Moyers told the president that he had sounded out Shriver about accepting the vice-presidential nomination and Shriver was agreeable and the Kennedy family had no objections. Moyers added that Shriver had said Bobby would have no complaint if Shriver was on the ticket.
>
> Johnson, grinning, looked at me questioningly. I leaned into the talk box and said, loud enough for Moyers to hear me, "The hell he wouldn't."

Moyers became quiet and Johnson laughed. Afterwards Kenny made clear to Johnson that any move to put Shriver on the ticket would be fought by the Kennedy factions of the party. "I made it plain. We felt that if any member of the late president's family was to be on the ticket, it should be Bobby. There is no substitute for Bobby, I explained. The Kennedys are not interchangeable. It is Bobby or no Kennedy at all. Johnson listened quietly. Then got up and got us both a drink. He said nothing more on the subject. With that the Shriver proposal was dropped."

If Kenny thought he had won the argument, though, he

would be proven to be wrong. The next day before lunch, Johnson called him into the office to discuss the issue once again.

"I've been thinking," Johnson said. "I think I need a Catholic on the ticket with me. How do you people feel about Gene McCarthy?"

Kenny was disgusted. "Listen, Mr. President, how can you pick the number two senator in Minnesota over the number one senator from the same state, Hubert Humphrey, who is better qualified and more strongly backed? It would be obvious that you were picking the number two man because he was a Catholic and Catholics would resent that."

While Johnson agreed with Kenny at the moment, Kenny said that in "his inscrutable way, [Johnson] sent Eugene McCarthy to see Mayor Daley in Chicago and Jesse Unruh in Los Angeles to sound out those Democratic leaders about getting delegate support at the convention."

Both Daley and Unruh knew Johnson had no serious intention of putting McCarthy on the ticket, but rather was continuing his political game with Bobby. Both leaders called Kenny as soon as the meeting with McCarthy ended. All agreed that they were disgusted that Johnson would not just "do the right thing," which, in their view, was to put Humphrey on the ticket.

"He will have to take him eventually," Kenny assured the two party leaders. "In the end, Lyndon wants to win and he will see he needs Hubert and our support to do that." Later, even McCarthy got upset with Johnson. He complained later to Kenny, "He never planned to take me. Why did he put me to that embarrassment?"

Still Johnson continued to insist he needed a Catholic on the ticket—any Catholic, that is, except for Bobby Kennedy. He went so far as to call a meeting of his political advisors in mid-April to share a poll he had read that showed he needed a Catholic on the ticket. When his advisors, which included Kenny, Larry O'Brien, Bill Moyers, Jack Valenti, Dick Maguire, Jim Rowe, and Walter Jenkins, dismissed the poll as biased and from a source that could not be relied upon, Johnson grew angry.

As Kenny remembered the conversation: "He expressed anger and amazement that all the Kennedy people present, all Catholics, disputed the findings of the poll and supported Humphrey. After the meeting broke up, Johnson was still upset and he called me alone into his office to argue the issue once again."

Johnson threw up his hands and said, "Well, if you want Humphrey that much, you can have him. You can leak it to the press right now that he's going to be my vice president and I won't deny it."

Kenny met Bobby later for drinks at Sans Souci. "Bobby and I agreed, we simply couldn't believe that Johnson would give up that easily; there had to be a catch somewhere."

Kenny explained later that he Bobby also agreed that they would not mention Johnson's offer to Humphrey, the press, or anybody else for that matter:

> We figured that if I leaked such a message to the press, Johnson might claim that the Kennedy people were forcing Humphrey on him, against his will, and that could be an excuse for him to drop Humphrey.
>
> We also understood Johnson well enough to know, if he was serious about accepting Humphrey on the ticket, he could and would spread the news himself instead of asking me to do it. If he wanted Humphrey on the ticket, he would want the credit for selecting him.
>
> Bobby and I decided to keep him guessing about Bobby's plans and intentions. Bobby's recent trips to Poland and Berlin

had been wildly acclaimed and only added to Johnson's anxieties and insecurities and deepened his suspicions of Bobby's intentions. We knew if we did this right, we could use this to our advantage, forcing his hand.

The next move proved to be Bobby's. As Kenny remembered it, "One night in May, Bobby invited a group of us to dinner at Hickory Hill to discuss his political situation."

The group included Bobby's brother Teddy, his brother-in-law Steve Smith, Larry O'Brien, Fred Dutton, and Kenny. After dinner they gathered for a few drinks down by the pool to continue the discussions. According to Kenny:

> Bobby told us that he had concluded that Barry Goldwater would win the Republican nomination, which meant Johnson would never invite him to share the Democratic ticket, and besides, he was certain after all these months that he simply could not work with Johnson. So, he had definitely decided to forget the vice presidency. He was planning to resign from the cabinet and go to New York immediately to begin a campaign there for Senate against Kenneth Keating.

Kenny was not entirely surprised. He, Bobby, and Jackie had been discussing plans for their next steps for some time. As Jackie had said back in Palm Beach during Christmas, whatever happened in the coming months would prove to be temporary for all of them.

Once Bobby had concluded that Johnson would do all he could to avoid having him on the ticket, and that, as the events of the previous months had shown without any doubt, he simply could not work with Johnson, he began in earnest to look for alternatives. He and Kenny had originally looked at the governorship in Massachusetts. Kenny had urged Bobby once again to run for it, knowing it would be an easy win for Bobby. But Bobby had decided he did not want to wait until the seat became available, especially when the Senate seat from New York was open right now.

Bobby also worried, as he told Kenny, "that if I run for governor in Massachusetts, I will overshadow Teddy and I am not sure that is fair to him." To Teddy's great relief, Bobby decided to look at the Senate seat in New York.

Like Bobby, Jackie was now looking to move to New York as well. She had found Washington, DC, a sad place filled with memories of Jack and what might have been. "I feel haunted here," she said. "I don't believe it is a healthy place for me and my children. There are just too many sad memories and might-have-beens."

With Bobby and Jackie decided, Kenny knew he would leave as well. "As soon as the election was over, I would resign and return to Massachusetts to run for governor, since Bobby had decided not to do so."

During the meeting at Hickory Hill, though, Kenny recalled, "Teddy and Steve urged Bobby to declare his candidacy for the Senate in New York as soon as possible." They feared Bobby would face heavy opposition in New York with charges of being a carpetbagger. Therefore, the sooner he announced and moved, the better in their view. "While politically I knew they were correct, I argued against such a move by Bobby. I asked Bobby not to announce his plans until we could build up a solid base of support that would force Johnson to take Humphrey. If you pull yourself out of the running, I argued, we would lose leverage on Johnson, and Johnson would feel free to pick a nonentity as his running mate."

While Bobby listened quietly, Teddy and Steve argued strongly against Kenny's suggestion. They felt Bobby had done enough and it was time for him to break free from Johnson, get to New York, announce his intentions, and put his all into the campaign.

"A vigorous argument between us developed," Kenny said. "Looking at it from Bobby's point of view, it was to his advantage to take himself out of the vice-presidential picture as soon as possible. Otherwise, it would appear later that he had decided to run for the Senate only as a last resort, after failing to get Johnson's invitation to be on the national ticket."

Kenny said, "Teddy argued correctly that Bobby was already on shaky ground running for the Senate seat from New York, a state where he had no roots of residency. And by delaying the announcement of his candidacy for the Senate until after we had gotten Humphrey the vice-presidential nomination, Bobby would open himself up to severe criticism and political harm."

While Kenny knew Teddy and Steve were right politically, and perhaps even emotionally, that the sooner Bobby headed to New York the better, he still argued in favor of Bobby waiting. Kenny pointed out that in order to have any control or voice in the Johnson administration, they would need to get Humphrey on board as the vice-presidential nominee and they could only do that if they could use Bobby's potential candidacy to force Johnson's hand.

Kenny said, "Under the circumstances, no realistic and shrewd politician would have listened to the plea I made on a strictly personal basis—that [Bobby] owed his brother's friends an obligation to do what he could to put a man with President Kennedy's liberal beliefs in the vice presidency. I told him, 'Listen, Bobby, Hubert is the best man available who represents those views. We have one shot with Johnson and only you have the power to force him to do the right thing.'"

The argument went back and forth, but in the end Bobby chose to listen to Kenny:

Senator John F. Kennedy, Pierre Salinger, and Kenneth P. O'Donnell during a campaign event, Michigan, October 26, 1960. *John F. Kennedy Library and Museum, Boston*

Robert F. Kennedy whispers something to Senate Majority Leader Lyndon Baines Johnson at the Democratic National Convention, July 1960. *AP Photo*

Senator Lyndon Baines Johnson and Senator John F. Kennedy on the front port of the Kennedy home in Hyannis Port on July 30, 1960. Inside the house is Kennedy aide Kenneth P. O'Donnell. *John F. Kennedy Library and Museum, Boston*

Lyndon Baines Johnson and John F. Kennedy pose during the 1960 presidential campaign. *John F. Kennedy Library and Museum, Boston*

Senators Johnson and Kennedy address journalists at a joint press conference from the Kennedy home, July 30, 1960. *Fay Foto Service, John F. Kennedy Library and Museum, Boston*

President John F. Kennedy and Kenneth P. O'Donnell, The White House, Washington, DC, 1962. *AP Photo*

President John F. Kennedy with Assistant Secretary of State for Far Eastern Affairs W. Averell Harriman in the Oval Office. *John F. Kennedy Library and Museum, Boston*

President John F. Kennedy, Kenneth P. O'Donnell, and Press Secretary Pierre Salinger visit Fort Bragg, North Carolina, 1961. *John F. Kennedy Library and Museum, Boston*

Vice President Lyndon Baines Johnson, Attorney General Robert F. Kennedy, and President John F. Kennedy discuss civil rights, Washington, DC, 1962. *AP Photo/ Charles Gorry*

President John F. Kennedy, Major General William C. Westmoreland, and Kenneth P. O'Donnell at a United States Military Academy ceremony, West Point, New York, 1962. *John F. Kennedy Library and Museum*

President Kennedy listens to Brig. Gen. Andrew J. Goodpaster, a White House aide during the Eisenhower Administration, as he calls on to say goodbye. Between them is Charles Spalding of New York, a friend of the President's. Kenneth P. O'Donnell, White House appointment secretary, is at left. Washington, DC, March 16, 1961. *AP Photo/Henry Burroughs*

Senator Edward M. Kennedy, Kenneth P. O'Donnell, Senator Robert F. Kennedy, and Speaker John McCormack at an O'Donnell for Governor event, Boston, 1966. *AP Photo/Bob Daugherty*

President Lyndon B. Johnson is sworn in aboard Air Force One with Jackie Kennedy and Kenneth P. O'Donnell, Love Field, Dallas, Texas, November 22, 1963. *John F. Kennedy Library and Museum, Boston*

Attorney General Robert F. Kennedy, Jackie Kennedy, and Kenneth P. O'Donnell deplane with John F. Kennedy's body, November 22, 1963. *AP Photo*

Special Assistant to the President Kenneth P. O'Donnell, The White House, Washington, DC. *John F. Kennedy Library and Museum, Boston*

Bobby agreed to put his own best interests aside and go along with my plan for delaying action because he felt that he had a personal responsibility to the party and to help Humphrey. To me, it was one of the finest and most unselfish decisions of Bobby's controversial career. Nobody realized the risk he took by agreeing to delay his announcement of his candidacy in New York. He put his own career at risk for the greater good. . . . As I was leaving Hickory Hill later that night, Bobby walked me to my car in his driveway and putting his arm on my shoulder, he said to me, "When they start the *ruthless brat* stuff, O'Donnell, you'd better be there to bleed along with me."

CHAPTER TWELVE

HARDBALL POLITICS

The next steps were clear as far as Kenny was concerned. "With Bobby keeping quiet about his plans, we were able to build up a solid base of support for Humphrey among Democratic state leaders and labor unions during the month of June."

From Kenny's viewpoint, the strategy was simple: "When then Republicans nominated Goldwater in July, leaving Johnson free to cut loose from Bobby, Humphrey was well fixed with influential backing, which meant Johnson would have no choice but to accept Humphrey."

Kenny said later that "Johnson's performance when he broke the news to Bobby caused some amusement in our circle." Kenny had arranged the meeting at Johnson's request in the Oval Office. He warned Bobby ahead of time to "select his words carefully, because Johnson usually recorded such conversations."

Kenny said their meeting was "short and sweet, filled with the usual tensions that were present in each meeting between the men. Johnson told Bobby he could not take him as vice president, providing this ridiculous explanation that he had decided to not include any of the cabinet members in his selection process." Bobby told Kenny later that Johnson had offered him various jobs in government, including that of Johnson's campaign manager. Bobby said he gritted his teeth at the offer, keeping in mind Kenny's warning that Johnson tended to record such conversations.

"But," Bobby said, "I turned it down, explaining to him that I had other plans, but I did not tell him what they involved. I wished him well and pledged my full support and then got the hell out of there as soon as possible."

Leaving the Oval Office, Bobby met Kenny and Larry O'Brien at Sans Souci for lunch. Bobby had walked down from the White House, hoping that the exercise would clear his head. After he sat down, he told Kenny and Larry "it was the first time since Jack died I felt free. I am not sure what kind of candidate I will make, but I feel finally on my own. I had to get out from under that man."

Bobby placed his own order and then began to fill them in on his conversation with Johnson. Kenny recalled that, "while Bobby was talking, a telephone was handed to me." The president was on the line.

"I just had a talk with your friend," he said.

"Mr. President, I want to be honest with you," Kenny said quickly. "The attorney general of the United States is sitting here with me right now."

There was momentary silence, but Johnson recovered quickly. "That's all right," Johnson said. "Can you come back over here? We've got to put out a statement."

Kenny left Bobby eating his lunch and discussing his Senate plans with Larry, then returned to the Oval Office. "I returned to the Oval Office, where Johnson gave me his version of a conversation with Bobby quite different from Bobby's version. Among other things, he said Bobby had practically begged to manage his campaign and was close to tears when Johnson turned him down."

"Mr. President," Kenny said sternly, his arms folded, giving Johnson that look that Jack Kennedy had dubbed "the stare," "I am sorry, Mr. President, the attorney general has told me just the opposite and knowing him as I do, I know he does not nor would he ever lie."

Johnson immediately stood and, in Kenny's words, "visibly bristled."

"He did, did he?" he said defensively. "Well, I'll bring Walter Jenkins in here and let him read you exactly what he did say."

As Kenny explained: "When the president asked Jenkins to read to us Bobby's conversation, he did not realize immediately, as Walter and I did, that he was revealing to me, and thus to Bobby and the Kennedy forces, that their talks had been recorded, as I had earlier told Bobby they would be."

Jenkins tried to shake the president off with "no" signals, but it took Johnson a few moments before he caught on. By then Kenny, Walter and, crucially, Johnson knew the damage had been done.

"What I meant to say, Walter," Johnson said fumbling, "was that I wanted you to read to us the notes on what I planned to say to Bobby." Then Johnson turned to Kenny, trying to cover himself, quickly saying, "You see, I had a feeling this meeting would be of some historical significance, so before Bobby came in here I wrote down exactly what I wanted to say to him."

Kenny nodded and decided to let it go. He had made his point and there was no sense, Kenny said later to his wife, "in continuing the farce."

In the end, Johnson was happy to be rid of Bobby, though still deeply fearful of Bobby's political power. And for his part Bobby was happy to be free of Johnson.

Kenny said later that when it came to "framing the announcement, Johnson decided on a Johnsonian dodge, which caused smiles all over Washington. He announced that he had made a ruling against selecting any member of the present cabinet, including of course the attorney general, as his vice-presidential nominee. That required us to get all of the other cabinet members, including Adlai Stevenson and Dean Rusk, to go through the same sham rigmarole, saying that they did not mind being disqualified for the vice presidency."

Bobby later remarked wryly, "I'm sorry to take so many nice fellows over the side with me."

For their part, Kenny, Bobby, and Larry were pleased Johnson had moved to take out the entire cabinet in order to "avoid looking like the villain for dumping Bobby."

The decision cleared the way and gave the Kennedy forces more room to maneuver their ultimate plan for the vice presidency—Hubert Humphrey.

Kenny wondered to his wife "just how much Johnson would have exploded if he had known that Bobby himself, a few months earlier, had decided against accepting the vice presidency under any conditions."

The same evening that Johnson released the statement dumping Bobby, Helen called Kenny at the White House. Hubert Humphrey had called the house and asked if Kenny would meet him at the Mayflower Hotel on Connecticut Avenue in Washington, DC, before he headed home. Kenny told Helen to call Humphrey back immediately and confirm the meeting. All communications with Humphrey had been conducted through Helen on their home telephone to ensure that Johnson did not get wind of their plans.

Kenny left the White House and headed quickly over to the hotel to meet quietly with Humphrey. His meeting was delayed briefly when he ran into an old reporter pal from the

Kennedy years. He invited Kenny to join the guys for dinner across the street at Duke Zeibert's restaurant. Kenny begged off and waited a few moments to be sure the coast was clear before heading into the bar to meet Humphrey.

"I went in there and met Humphrey in the back of the bar. We had a private table in the back. We ordered a couple drinks and I told him Bobby just got the axe. I said, Hubert, you're next unless you are willing to put up a fight to get the nomination."

"I will do that, Kenny," Hubert said, "but only if you can assure me that the Kennedy people would support me in a floor fight."

Kenny told Hubert that the Kennedy people were behind him completely, saying, "You have my word and Bobby's as well. He's authorized me to tell you as much."

With that assurance in place, Hubert agreed to make the fight. He said later he knew Kenny well enough to know that "If Kenny gives you his word, you can take it to the bank. So I knew I could take the next step."

The next step was getting the United Auto Workers and their president, Walter Reuther, squarely on board behind Humphrey's candidacy for the vice presidency. The next day Kenny met Reuther's top political aide and his long-time friend Jack Conway for drinks at the same private table at the Mayflower Hotel. Conway agreed with Kenny's plan and assured him that "he and Walter would work to get an endorsement from labor for Humphrey as the vice-presidential nominee."

"If [Johnson] wants a floor fight," Conway said, "this time we will give him one. He cannot win without us."

With two more pieces of the political puzzle falling into place, Kenny continued his efforts to press ahead. He moved stealthily and put all the Kennedy forces behind Humphrey.

In his role as executive director of both the campaign and the Democratic National Committee, Kenny was in a unique position to reach out to all the necessary Kennedy forces without raising too much suspicion around Johnson or his people.

"It was no small feat," Kenny remarked, "since my friendship with Bobby made me always suspect. Despite his meeting with Bobby, the president remained unconvinced that Bobby would truly stay out of the nomination fight. This meant my actions continued to be scrutinized. But we were able to move quietly and quickly, often using my wife Helen as the go-between to avoid calls to me at the White House. The idea was to put everything in place, leaving the president no choice or room to maneuver."

The day after Kenny's meeting with Jack Conway, Bobby made his move. Kenny said, "I had prearranged a meeting that was nevertheless designed to look spontaneous at least to Johnson." Bobby went up to meet with Humphrey at his Senate office.

With everything planned in advance, Kenny said, "In front of cameras Bobby went up and put his arm around Hubert to announce to the press that Hubert Humphrey was his choice for the vice presidency." As planned, the move caught Johnson completely off guard as he watched the coverage from his multiple televisions in the Oval Office.

Kenny recalled, "That startled Johnson and he was further startled when he was hit right after that by a barrage of prearranged Humphrey endorsements from several state governors—Hughes of Iowa, Brown of California, and Reynolds of Wisconsin, among others. And from such labor leaders as Reuther, George Meaney, and David Dubinsky."

Johnson was reportedly furious with Kenny, Bobby, and Humphrey, but unsure of what steps to take to counter their political moves.

"As the pressure mounted on Johnson," Kenny confirmed, "he became resentful and peevish":

> He treated Humphrey roughly at White House legislative meetings and Washington social affairs, often asking him in front of a group of people, including members of the press, what he, Humphrey, thought of Sarge Shriver or Eugene McCarthy or even Tom Dodd as a vice-presidential possibility.
>
> For his part, Hubert was careful. He held his tongue and asked supporters not to press Johnson too hard or to humiliate him. He was mindful of our larger strategy. He recognized, as did Johnson, that we had a lock on the vice presidency on Hubert's behalf. Hubert wanted to be careful to not cause too much public embarrassment to Johnson. . . .
>
> The choice of Humphrey was more or less unavoidable, but the president kept him in doubt, or at least tried to, right up until the last possible moment on the day when the delegates at the convention were to vote on the nomination, insisting to reporters that his mind was not made up.

As much as Johnson tried to embarrass Humphrey, Humphrey seemed to understand it all. "He was more tolerant than I would have been," Bobby remarked later.

"We've got to give him the sense that he still has options," Humphrey cautioned Kenny. Always a wily legislator, Humphrey warned the Kennedy people, "Let's not publicly box him in too much. He has to feel it is his decision."

Johnson, dubbed by the press the "master of the Senate," was not as easily outflanked as Kenny and Bobby believed he could be. As the walls began to close in, Johnson understood that Kenny, with Bobby's blessing, had outmaneuvered him politically. As Walter Jenkins relayed to Kenny, "[Johnson] was not happy. He felt that Bobby had once again gotten the better of him. It infuriated him."

Nevertheless, Kenny, along with the other Kennedy forces, prepared to arrive in Atlantic City the week before the convention, confident in their belief that Humphrey was assured the vice presidency whether Johnson liked it or not.

As it turned out, they had greatly underestimated Lyndon Johnson. "During the week before the convention, Johnson pulled a move that surprised us all," Kenny said later with a chuckle, perhaps marveling at being outmaneuvered so deftly. "Johnson made one last stab at dropping Humphrey and picking somebody else whom even Humphrey's supporters would have hesitated to oppose—Mike Mansfield, the Senate majority leader.

"We were stunned. It never crossed my mind," Kenny said. "None of us working in the White House suspected that Johnson was considering Mansfield until the senator from Montana was mentioned as a likely vice-presidential candidate in a column by William S. White, the newspaper commentator who was one of Johnson's closest Texan friends."

White was used often by Johnson to float a "political kite," as Kenny put it, to see which way the wind was blowing on any given issue. "The mention of Mansfield in his column was a clear indication that Johnson was still trying to ditch Humphrey," Kenny said.

A few days later, Kenny was at home in Washington packing his bags and preparing to leave for the convention. "I was fielding calls from the Humphrey people, labor, and from Bobby as he mapped out his thoughts on a speech about his brother," he said.

In the midst of all these calls, the red phone in the O'Donnell kitchen rang. It could only mean one thing: the president was calling. Kenny hung up from Bobby and went down to pick up the call. Before he could say a word, Johnson began.

"Listen, Kenny," he said, "I still think we have to have a Catholic on the ticket," making no mention of Humphrey.

"Mr. President," Kenny said, "I thought we agreed that Hubert Humphrey was going to be the vice president."

"You agreed," Johnson said slyly. "And besides, agreements come and go. The most important thing is that we get the presidency. I've decided on Mike Mansfield."

Kenny stood in silence. Mansfield was not only a Kennedy man, but he was Kenny's close friend and Johnson knew it.

"Look, Kenny," Johnson continued, "you can't be against Mansfield. You, Bobby, nor any of the Kennedy people. He's one of you. You admire him and respect him. If you're thinking of Bobby running for president in 1972, Mansfield's no problem. He'll be too old to run then."

Rather weakly, Kenny said, "Mr. President, I don't think Mike Mansfield will take the nomination." Though as he said it, the truth was Kenny was bluffing. He had never thought of Mansfield for the vice presidency, so he had no idea one way or the other. Had the president already gotten Mansfield to agree? Kenny had no idea.

"Let me tell you something," the president said. "That's what they said about old Lyndon Johnson in 1960. But when they lead you up on that mountain and show you those green fields down below and that beautiful White House standing there—you know what you do? You take it. They all take it."

"Then" Kenny recalled, having made his point, "without saying another word, [Johnson] hung up. I stood there holding the line. I was admittedly speechless. He had us and we both knew it."

Kenny finished packing and prepared to leave for Atlantic City. "What do you think is going to happen?" Helen asked him as they walked to the car and waited for his driver to take his bag.

Kenny was silent for a moment. Helen thought he seemed more thoughtful than concerned.

"Let's not say anything about the conversation with the president for now. Not even to Bobby."

Helen was puzzled, but agreed. She had learned to trust his political instincts.

"I went to Atlantic City," Kenny said. "I heard nothing there about Mike Mansfield being nominated for vice president. I never mentioned my conversation with the president to anyone until a few years later, when I met with Mike Mansfield about something else entirely. When we finished our business conversation I was unable to contain my curiosity any longer, and I asked what had happened between he and Johnson in 1964. Mansfield took the pipe out of his mouth and smiled."

"I, too, saw White's column," Mansfield told Kenny, "and like everybody else in Washington I knew what it meant. I waited a while and then I decided to beat Johnson to the punch. I went to the White House and I said to him, 'Mr. President, I saw Mr. White's column in the newspaper, and I want you to know that under no circumstances will I ever accept the nomination for vice president.' That ended that."

In the end, Kenny and Bobby's strategy would succeed— Johnson would be forced to select Hubert Humphrey as his vice-presidential nominee. However, Kenny noted, in true "Johnsonian style" he played games with Humphrey right up until the end:

> Rather childishly, or sadistically, Johnson kept Humphrey in suspense even when he invited Humphrey to the White House from Atlantic City on the Wednesday of convention week, supposedly to be given the vice-presidential nod.
>
> Johnson asked Tom Dodd to come to Washington on the same day, even arranging for the two senators to fly on

the same plane. Humphrey and a group of his supporters wondered if Johnson was switching to Dodd, despite everything, at the last minute. There was no way to tell and it was too late to alert supporters at the convention.

The two men arrived at the White House together. Johnson saw Dodd first and kept Humphrey waiting in another room for over an hour, even going so far as to make sure that Dodd left through a different door, so that he and Humphrey would not be able to speak before Johnson saw Humphrey. Even when Johnson finally did see Humphrey he continued the foolishness.

He kept Humphrey waiting for well over an hour, when he finally called him in, he had Humphrey sit across from him on the other side of his desk in the Oval Office. He went through a lengthy description of what he expected from his vice president, and what the duties and obligations of the vice presidency involved. He must be a Johnson man down to the tips of his toes, and he must do whatever Johnson asked him to; he must be able to share secrets that no man would know; he must be prepared for special duties in space, education, civil rights, welfare, and agriculture.

After this lengthy monologue, Johnson finally said, "If you didn't know that I had you picked a month ago, maybe you haven't got brains enough to be the vice president."

Not for the first time nor the last, Hubert Humphrey bit his tongue. When he left the White House he called Kenny and confirmed the news: "It is done. You can tell Bobby I said thank you and go ahead."

A ceremony followed Johnson and Humphrey's meeting. First there was a ceremony in the cabinet room, then a presidential call to Muriel Humphrey in Atlantic City, and then a press conference at the White House.

"Afterwards," as Robert Novak reported at the time, "everyone went upstairs in the White House where there was laid out plenty of drinks and food for all White House aides, reporters, and both members of the Democratic committee's national ticket. Johnson was gay, exuberant, teasing, and understandably self-satisfied." For the first time in a while, at least momentarily, he felt free of Bobby Kennedy.

In Atlantic City, Kenny had hung up from Humphrey and placed his next call to Bobby Kennedy. Their plan had succeeded. John Kennedy's man was in the number two spot in the White House.

"Somewhere up there your brother is smiling," Kenny told Bobby. Bobby was quiet for a moment. "I think so," he said softly. "I hope so."

Now the two friends eyed the Senate seat in New York. It was time for Bobby to take the next step.

CHAPTER THIRTEEN
THE PRESIDENT

Lyndon Johnson's next move was on Kenny, and it caught both him and Bobby by surprise.

"Johnson called me into his office," Kenny recalled, "and told me he was sending me over to the Democratic National Committee. He wanted me to take John Bailey's job as chairman."

Kenny later admitted to Bobby and Helen that he had been caught off guard. "I even called Larry [O'Brien] to see if he had heard about this. I knew Johnson enjoyed bouncing ideas off Larry. But he was as surprised as I was."

The next time Johnson and Kenny talked about the potential change, Kenny was more prepared:

I told him that I would not take John Bailey's job as national chairman. Bailey was my friend. He was President Kennedy's friend and you don't do those kind of things. He then offered me Dick Maguire's job as treasurer. I told him both my wife and my sister, who worked for Maguire, would say that would be a dangerous place to put me.

The president laughed like hell and so did I. We had a

drink and that broke the ice. Then we agreed I would go over as executive director and at his insistence split my time between my current post as special assistant to the president in the White House and also take on full-time duties as executive director.

When I first told Bobby he was upset and thought somehow it was his fault. Bobby always took on the blame himself for everybody.

Kenny said Bobby laughed. "Come on, Bobby," he told him, "You cannot blame the guy. He wants his own people. They are sharp and talented. He doesn't need me. He knows while I am always honest with him, that my first loyalty is to you. He also knows that we shoved Humphrey down his throat and someone has to pay a price. That's politics. Your brother would be no different."

"Bobby always worried about the other person first," Helen said. "But the truth was that Kenny was, I think, happy to be out of that building and away from the Oval Office." Kenny admitted as much to Jackie, telling her that "there were just too many memories." He also said to her, "Once Johnson is safely reelected, now that you and Bobby are safely off to New York, Helen and I will return to Massachusetts and politics there."

Jackie was against the idea, trying unsuccessfully to convince Kenny to go to New York and work with Bobby. "Maybe he should have," Kenny's sister Justine said later, "but he was haunted that he had let the president down in Dallas and he felt, incorrectly I believe, that Bobby needed new people of his own."

Part of Kenny's job—the same job he had held during the 1960 campaign—involved scheduling Johnson in places that did the most good not just for Johnson, but for down-ballot candidates who could ride on Johnson's coattails.

As Kenny explained:

Running against Goldwater was so easy and Johnson's instincts were very good, so Bailey and I had little to do. Goldwater was just a terrible candidate. So Bailey and I spent a lot of time talking on the telephone to kill time and the only race we really focused on was Bobby's Senate run. The major challenge we had there was, besides Bobby's weakness as a candidate—a role he simply was not accustomed to—but our main concern was keeping the Johnson people and certain members of that group from sabotaging Bobby's campaign. There was a determined effort to do so and we worked hard to cut them off before they could cause any real harm. Whether this was directed by President Johnson or not, I cannot be clear, but he likely knew about the efforts and allowed them to continue.

"He doesn't want me in the Senate either," Bobby complained to Kenny during a break in one of their political meetings at Hickory Hill.

Kenny laughed. "What do you expect, Bobby? He saw that seventeen-minute ovation for you in Atlantic City. He sees the crowds. He knows you remain, whether in the cabinet or the Senate, his most substantial political threat in the Democratic Party."

While Bobby agreed, he said, "I guess I felt once I was off to New York and the Senate, he would feel less threatened."

Kenny shook his head at what he saw as Bobby's political naiveté. "In the Senate you will build your own political base just as your brother did. It provides you with your own platform to promote your ideas and agenda. He cannot stand the idea of it," Kenny said. Bobby nodded. He sipped his milk and stared out the window for a moment.

"His agenda," Bobby repeated. It took Kenny a moment to realize that Bobby was not talking about Johnson, but about his brother. Even as he stood potentially poised to win the Senate seat, Bobby saw himself still only in terms of carrying forth his brother Jack's unfinished agenda.

"Maybe," Kenny admitted to his sister Justine later, "that is how they all saw themselves—as carrying on John Kennedy's agenda."

Justine remembered she just listened. She had not been sure what to say, but she hoped that Kenny would either stay on with Johnson or go with Bobby to New York. "I did not feel good about his returning to Massachusetts, but I recognized we would all do what he felt was best."

Kenny admitted later that the "truth was Johnson was not particularly anxious to have Bobby in the Senate with his own power base. I knew Bobby was correct about that, but I did not want Bobby to focus on Johnson, but rather look towards his future, not his past."

"You should take your own advice," Bobby teased Kenny one evening in New York as they sat with John Bailey having drinks at Toots Shor's Restaurant. Kenny laughed softly and shrugged, still staring forward.

"Yeah, I know," Kenny said. "But let's get you underway first and then worry about everybody else later."

Bobby nodded in agreement.

After a few moments of silence Bobby said, "I just don't know if I can be as good at this as he was." They all continued to sip their drinks in silence for a few moments.

"I think," Kenny said, "if I don't presume too much, he would say to you what he told me once about you."

"Which was?" Bobby asked. He stared at Kenny almost anxiously, his tie loose and hair an uncombed mess.

"He said you were the smartest and best damn fellow he

ever knew," Kenny said. "And even if you weren't his brother, he would want you to have his back."

Bobby stared at Kenny for a moment, allowing the words to sink in.

"Then," Kenny quipped, "he'd tell you to straighten your damn tie and comb your hair."

They all laughed.

"Bobby was a very different Kennedy than his brother," John Bailey said later. "Maybe that made him even more of a concern to the White House. He was in many ways a far less traditional and predictable politician. I think Johnson really didn't know quite what to make of him."

Kenny recalled that Johnson's friends were active in New York working for Kenneth Keating, Bobby's Republican opponent.

Until John Bailey and I got wind of it and stopped them, they even tried to open a Johnson headquarters in New York City instead of a Johnson-Kennedy headquarters. This was never done in national politics that way. Bailey and I were going to have none of it.

One day I was sitting in my office at the Democratic National Committee headquarters and a Johnson man called me frantically from a hotel room in New York, where two of Bobby's workers imported from Massachusetts, Matty Ryan and my younger brother, Warren, were threatening to throw the fellow out a window unless he agreed to schedule the president for an appearance in Brooklyn with Bobby during the last week of the campaign.

Maybe the wisest thing for you to do, I said to him, would be to schedule the president for Brooklyn. After all, Matty and Warren are a couple of strong husky boys and Warren has kind of a short fuse. A half-hour later the president called me from Denver. He was furious.

He said to me, "I am not going to Brooklyn to take care of your friend Bobby Kennedy."

Kenny listened for a moment while the president let off steam and then said, "Mr. President, forget it. If you go to Brooklyn with Bobby, everybody in the crowd will be looking at and cheering for you instead of him, so it won't do him much good."

Johnson was silent for a moment and then hung up without a word. The next day he called and indicated he had changed his schedule of his planned tour of New York and was going to Brooklyn with Bobby. Kenny said., "I listened and said, 'Gee, Mr. President, I wish you wouldn't, you will overshadow him.'"

The two men appeared together in Brooklyn for their first real major campaign appearance. "It was an enormous crowd even though there was a World Series game on television that night," Kenny remembered. "The crowd was screaming Bobby's name and pushing and pulling try to get close to the two men. Later Bobby asked me how I got Johnson to agree. I smiled and said, 'You don't want to know.' Bobby, knowing me as he did, said, 'Yeah, you know what? That is probably true.'"

"As a presidential campaigner," Kenny reported, "Johnson pulled several boners that the politically astute John Kennedy never would have committed, but fortunately for him the 1964 fight against Goldwater was such a pushover that his mistakes did him no real harm." An example of what Kenny considered a rookie mistake was when Johnson decided to go to Delaware to attack Senator John Williams, who had exposed the influence peddling scheme of Johnson protégé Bobby Baker.

"We were sitting in the Oval Office going over the schedule and [Johnson] announced his intention to go to campaign against Williams in Delaware, which was Williams's home state. I said to him," Kenny recalled, "'Mr. President, don't go to Delaware. Reporters there will ask you questions about Williams and the Baker case. Your attacks and presence there will only stir up damaging headlines about the Baker scandal. Why put yourself in that position?'"

Johnson got up red-faced and told Kenny angrily, "Listen, Kenny, I want to go to Delaware and screw that bastard for what he did to poor Bobby Baker, who is my friend. I am president. Just do it."

Kenny said little more about the situation to the president, but solved the issue another way. "I kept him out of Delaware by making sure to schedule the only possible day he could go there would be a Sunday. So on a Sunday, I deliberately scheduled Johnson to be in Delaware, but Johnson was at the LBJ Ranch in Texas and not budging. He called me furious from the ranch."

"Kenny, you make me mad. I know you did that on purpose," he growled through the phone.

Kenny just laughed. "Yes, Mr. President, I did and you will eventually thank me for it."

Johnson slammed the telephone down in anger, but he never did go to Delaware and he made it through the election without the Baker scandal ever becoming an issue.

It seemed Johnson had laid down two firm rules when it came to his campaign scheduling. He had made clear he would not campaign on Sundays, and he would never campaign in his opponent's home state, simply as a matter of courtesy. Kenny told Bobby he thought it was nuts. "Your brother would never miss an opportunity to campaign for votes anytime or anywhere."

In the midst of his own campaign Bobby was mystified as well, saying to Kenny, "I can understand his reluctance to appear in Goldwater's home state of Arizona, a waste of time anyway, but his refusal to campaign on Sundays is baffling to me. Jack always said Sundays were his big days on the campaign trail."

Kenny agreed with Bobby, but when he tried to push Johnson, the president refused. "Kenny, listen," Johnson explained, "religious Southerners frown on campaigning on Sundays."

Kenny had never heard such nonsense. When he asked members of the Southerner delegation, they knew nothing about it. One senator said to Kenny, "Oh, Lyndon just makes stuff up. You know that."

Kenny just shook his head and had to laugh. He admitted, "These were small issues, but things I would never have dealt with under John Kennedy. Lyndon could just be baffling to me sometimes."

But Kenny admitted later:

It was a relief to see Lyndon Johnson safely elected on his own to the White House and taking over the presidency with a solid feeling of security after the unhappy months of trying to fill out the remainder of John Kennedy's unfinished term and working uncomfortably with Kennedy's cabinet and Kennedy's White House staff. He had wanted to be a good president, when he was serving in the office as a stand-in for his dead predecessor, but he was always uncomfortably aware that most of the Kennedy-appointed people around him, particularly the Eastern Ivy Leaguers from the New Frontier administration, were cool towards him and regarded his presence in the White House as an unhappy accident. He was striving to do his best under unpleasant circumstances, and his situation was a hard one. . . .

At times I felt very sorry for him and I was unhappy about the way he was treated. I particularly remember one evening that spring when all of us at the White House were invited to a cocktail party for Jacqueline Kennedy at the F Street Club. The president asked Larry O'Brien and me rather anxiously if we would go to the party with him. When we arrived at the club, we found that the three of us were the only men in business suits. Everyone else was dressed in formal evening attire. They were all going later to a formal embassy dinner that the president had not been invited to attend. All the guests were swarming around Jackie Kennedy, who looked radiant and happy to be making her first formal social appearance since her husband's funeral, and nobody, and I mean nobody, was paying any attention to Johnson. He stood there in the corner in this rather baggy suit with a drink in his hand while all the swells swarmed around Jackie and Bobby, who both looked like movie stars. I stood in the corner with the president, not wanting to leave him alone, and I had a drink with him while he quietly watched the scene.

After a moment he said to me, "I guess all of them are going someplace special for dinner. Are you going with them?"

Kenny had been invited, but seeing the scene unfold decided to take a pass. He said none of that to Johnson, but instead told him, "No, Mr. President, I have nothing planned."

Johnson seemed relieved. Turning to Kenny, he said, "Good. Would you mind coming back to the White House with me? We can have a drink and dinner there."

Kenny told him he would be delighted. They quietly left the room without anyone taking any notice of either their arrival or departure. As they drove back to the White House, Johnson finally turned to him and said, "Despite what they think, I am still President of the United States. I didn't want it this way."

Kenny shook his head. "Mr. President, ignore them. People handle situations differently. I would let it roll off your back."

Johnson stared at Kenny for a long moment. "You wouldn't," he said.

Kenny shrugged and after a moment admitted as much.

"No, Mr. President, I probably wouldn't."

When Kenny got home, despite the late hour, he called Bobby and gave him hell.

"Like it or not, he is president of the United States. You owe him some respect."

Bobby was embarrassed and admitted he got caught up in the moment. "I will call and apologize," Bobby assured Kenny. Whether he did or not, Kenny never knew and didn't want to ask.

Kenny admitted later, "Sadly, there were many moments like that for Johnson. What I hoped for him with this landslide victory over Goldwater in November '64 was that he could come into his own. Be his own man and focus on what he wanted to do, especially with civil rights and the social 'safety-net,' as he called it. While I did not plan to stay, I wanted him to finally stand free of the shadow of his predecessor. I just hoped he could finally become a president in his own right and under his own terms."

"The presidential race in 1964 was a contest not just for victory for the Democrats, for Johnson's victory was assured on July 16 at the Republican National Convention in San Francisco," reported the national political press at the time. But the very moment the Republican Party's right wing seized control of the party for the first time since 1924, ignored the consensus, and nominated Barry Goldwater, of Arizona, the result was assured, reported Rowland Evans and Bob Novak in their column.

Once Goldwater was the nominee, Kenny said, "Bobby

and I knew that Johnson was assured a landslide it was only a question of how large a landslide. So that is why Bobby, John Bailey, and I focused on Bobby's election to the Senate, while Larry O'Brien focused on Johnson."

Finally, Lyndon Johnson had gained full control of the Democratic Party. He had accomplished it himself, in his own unique way.

CHAPTER FOURTEEN
THE CAMPAIGN

The Republican nominee, Barry Goldwater, senator from Arizona, was running not only against Johnson but also against the ghost of John F. Kennedy and the tragedy of Dallas. It is doubtful that any Republican nominee would have had much of a chance, but certainly not Goldwater, who was beaten almost two-to-one in public-opinion polls among his own party's rank and file by Governor William Scranton of Pennsylvania, his last opponent for the nomination for president.

Goldwater was, as Rowland Evans described him, "the voice of the renascent Republican right, he was the antithesis of Lyndon Johnson: uninterested in power, inflexible doctrinaire, essentially nonpolitical. He was, in short, everything a candidate for president of the United States should not be. All these weaknesses had been aggravated by his unsuccessful Republican foes, who had planted in the public mind the caricature of Barry Goldwater as a political Neanderthal who would risk nuclear war and abolish the Social Security system."

Johnson understood full well that no miracle could save Goldwater. But once the Republican Party had done the unthinkable and nominated him, Johnson became a man possessed with ambition not just to win, and not just to win handsomely, but to win the largest presidential victory in the history of the country. As early in the race as January, Larry O'Brien and Kenny had discussed the potential size of Johnson's landslide if some order could be brought to the chaos that currently enveloped Johnson's campaign.

"Larry was one of the shrewdest students of Democratic politics and history in the business," Kenny insisted. "He told Johnson point blank that he [Johnson] could exceed Franklin Roosevelt's 63 percent of the popular vote in 1936, or even Warren Harding's 64 percent in 1920."

Frankly, Johnson was skeptical at first, but his respect for O'Brien was so complete that he was loath to dismiss him out of hand. "I think at first he was skeptical of what Larry was saying," Kenny said, "but once [Larry] laid out the numbers and the history, Johnson got it. It went without saying that it was the circumstances of John Kennedy's death that put Johnson in such a strong position vis-à-vis the race. Johnson understood that, though he was careful not to say it too often."

Robert Novak said, "Not until they understood it did his aides and advisors also understand how a candidate so far ahead as Johnson was could fret and worry as much as Johnson did in the 1964 campaign."

"Larry had laid out these numbers for Johnson and that became his goalpost," Kenny said. "He did not want to just win, but he wanted to win by a margin such as Roosevelt or Harding had done. That became his goal."

"A landslide would be the last and mightiest step in his consolidation of power," Evans and Novak wrote. They explained that as Johnson saw it, "he had survived the crisis of confidence during the transition, put the stamp of the Great Society on his administration, disposed of the Bobby Problem, and dictated the one-man convention at Atlantic City. Here now was the final goal: to win by so large a margin that the consensus he sought as the means to power would be ratified by an unprecedented electoral landslide. That was the goal."

"Larry was the shrewdest guy in politics," Kenny confirmed, "but it doesn't do a damn bit of good to be smart as hell, if your candidate won't listen to you. We were not Johnson men, but we had to find a way to get him to listen to our strategy and plan if he wanted to win by that 64 percent margin."

The problem was that the Johnson campaign was disorganized, tactics unsettled, and the plan to victory was as murky as it had been in 1960 when Johnson was trying to wrestle the nomination away from Kennedy. "Johnson made mistakes that John Kennedy would never have made. His organization was a mess and there were people there that Bobby Kennedy would never have tolerated in the Kennedy campaign. That said," Kenny continued, "if Larry's strategy could be put into play, given the nation's emotion around the ghost of John Kennedy, we believed that despite the Johnson disarray we could still come in around 64 percent."

"What difference does that make?" Bobby asked Kenny during dinner in New York late one evening. "Bobby was deeply involved in his own situation now," Kenny said later. "So Johnson's margin was not foremost on his mind. I understood that completely."

"I want to leave him in the best possible position," Kenny said to Bobby. "I think if Larry and I can achieve that, then we can leave here in January feeling as though we did the right thing and that Johnson can take the ball and run with it from there."

Bobby nodded. Then he stared for a while out the window silently. "I know you are right," Bobby agreed. "As we said before it is the right thing to do. My brother would be pleased;

that said, I still wish things had gone differently. But I will do whatever you need me to do to help."

Kenny could only nod in reply. There was little else to say. Finally, he added, "We are where we are now. We have to do what must be done." Bobby nodded again and then chuckled.

Trying perhaps to lighten his own darkening mood, Bobby teased Kenny, saying, "You better not tell him that you are having dinner with me again and I agreed to help, then he will never trust your judgment."

Kenny laughed. "He doesn't trust it now. That is why I do most of my talking through O'Brien. That seems to work okay. He listens to Larry."

"Unless you are Larry," Bobby added with a laugh. The two friends chuckled.

"It was a difficult time," Kenny admitted later. "Our emotions were still so raw, and the problems between Bobby and Johnson were getting more difficult each day, and often the conflicts were very petty on both their parts, really. It was a difficult time for all of us on many levels. I think Larry maybe handled it the best of us all."

The week before President John Kennedy went to Dallas in 1963, the first pre-campaign meeting was held at the White House. "President Kennedy was hoping to profit by the invaluable experience of the cliff-hanger against Nixon in 1960. We were building the best-oiled, most efficient political organization of all time a whole year before the 1964 election," Kenny explained. Bobby was too busy with his duties as attorney general to attend, therefore brother-in-law Stephen Smith was to take over as campaign manager. O'Brien held the same job he had in 1960: director of organization, dealing with state party leaders. "I would have had the same duties as I had in the 1960 campaign, but this time including dealing with troublesome states that had been close or lost in 1960. By the time we left for Dallas the campaign was an ongoing concern. All this machinery was in place or prepared to be in place when Johnson took over. He could have just stepped into place," Kenny said.

But Johnson did not do that, at least not in the way the Kennedy men had hoped he would. Bob Novak recalled, "Johnson had other concerns and other ways of going about politics. Kennedy's ambitious plan was forgotten. Johnson had not even named a campaign manager by the time the convention rolled around. Even in Atlantic City at the convention he had no director of organization. His campaign organization or strategy was really disorganization and it defied schematic description."

In the end, Johnson told Kenny over drinks one night, "I cannot decide who I want to be my campaign manager, so I think it will just be good old Lyndon Johnson and my gut." Kenny explained to Johnson that John Kennedy would never make that mistake. Johnson just shook his head in reply. "Kenny, I am not John Kennedy. I know you loved him, but I do things in my own way. I am asking you to learn the Johnson way."

Later that evening Kenny confessed to his wife that he was not at all sure he could make the transition. "I don't think I can be a Johnson man," Kenny said. "I think I just don't understand his approach. I don't want to hold him back. But I think Larry seems better able to communicate with him."

When Kenny caught up with Bobby in New York a few days later, he related the conversation. He confessed to Bobby he was appalled. He saw such a decision as both amateurish and dangerous.

Kenny said, "I don't see how he can lose given that his opponent is Goldwater, but if he truly wants 64 percent and to win over the country in his own right, every good campaign needs a strong, capable campaign manager."

Bobby agreed, but joked that "despite his offering me the job I am busy with my own campaign."

Kenny laughed. The idea that Johnson had even asked Bobby to take such a job still made both Kenny and Bobby annoyed, though Johnson seemed to have long forgotten it.

"I think he just cannot stand to do anything in the manner my brother did things," Bobby said. "Kenny, just do whatever you need to do. If Larry can run point and, more importantly, Johnson is willing let him, then let Larry do it. Let it go," Bobby advised. "Besides you have my Senate race to worry about." Kenny chuckled. He knew Bobby was of course correct.

Johnson did not agree with Kenny's approach to the campaign, and while he liked Kenny personally, he felt Kenny didn't understand his approach.

"He knows how to do things the Kennedy way," Johnson said, "but that is not my way." Johnson was still haunted by the ghost of John Kennedy and now Bobby Kennedy. So that was in no small part why he sent Kenny over to the Democratic National Committee. Johnson realized that over there Kenny would focus most of his attention on Bobby's race in New York.

""Look," Johnson told Kenny, "I know you are going to spend most of your time as executive director working for Bobby Kennedy in New York, so that is fine as long as you come when I call. I want you to keep your hand in at the White House. But you will be set up over there. I know you want to help Bobby as much, maybe more, than you want to help me. God knows he needs the help."

Kenny had laughed. "I think I could hardly blame him. In truth, I may have been as relieved as he was with the decision," Kenny confessed.

The inner workings of the Johnson campaign were as far from the well-oiled Kennedy machine as one could imagine. It was reported that speechwriters came and went, sometimes in the course of a day.

Bob Novak wrote, "Most prominent inside the government were four White House aides—Bill Moyers, Richard Goodwin, Horace Busby, and Douglas Carter. Johnson also enlisted the assistance of close friend Secretary of Labor Willard Wirtz, a close Johnson friend, but his role was held in deepest secrecy so as not to offend those other aides in the White House."

On top of what the national political press dubbed a "madcap campaign," Larry O'Brien had an additional position; he was director of organization of the campaign—the same job he had held under Kennedy. However, in 1964 there was no Johnson organization to direct since the campaign was in such disarray. When O'Brien managed to finally free himself of his duties as chief congressional lobbyist for the administration, it was already September. Despite this, O'Brien quickly fell into the role as another high-level agent for Johnson.

"Larry became, in my view," Kenny admitted, "a vital link between Johnson, the Democratic Committee, and the Kennedys. Bobby may have been running for senator in New York, but outside of Johnson, Bobby remained the most powerful Democrat in the country. Johnson understood he simply could not afford to have a public feud with Bobby. It annoyed Johnson, but he was a political realist. He wanted to win and win in his own right as president."

"I am not kowtowing to Bobby," Johnson warned Kenny bluntly one evening over drinks at the White House.

Kenny nodded. "I understand, Mr. President, and so does he," Kenny said, hoping to defuse any further discussion of Bobby.

Johnson sat thoughtfully for a moment, nursing his drink. "Well good," he said, "but I am not really sure I believe you."

Kenny was in an impossible position. He got along very well with Johnson for the most part. In fact, he was serving in a critical transition role as Johnson built up his self-confidence, stepped into his own as president, and began to get his own men around him. That said, Kenny knew Johnson's insecurity around Bobby and the Kennedys meant Johnson could never completely trust him. Kenny's long friendship with Bobby and John Kennedy and his deep loyalty to them would always make him suspect in Johnson's eyes as long as Johnson was convinced Bobby was a threat.

"I will be glad when January comes," Kenny confessed to Helen. "I dislike being caught in between Johnson and Bobby."

His wife understood, but she had her own worries. With Bobby off running for Senate in New York, Jackie moving to New York, and Kenny not planning to stay on with Johnson, their future was uncertain. Secretly she hoped Kenny would stay and go to work for Bobby in the Senate, but Bobby was trying to convince Kenny to return to Massachusetts and run for governor in 1966.

Helen thought it was a terrible idea and tried to convince Bobby of that in numerous conversations, but this time her entreaties did not succeed.

"If he is not coming with me to the Senate," Bobby told her, "I think becoming governor of Massachusetts is a great plan."

But Helen was not the only one who thought it a terrible idea. So did Teddy Kennedy, who was busy trying to consolidate his own power in the state much as Jack Kennedy had done in 1952. Ted Kennedy wanted a governor he could control. He knew that was not Kenny O'Donnell.

With all these varying agendas afoot during the campaign year of 1964, Kenny, Bobby and Johnson increasingly found that Larry O'Brien was a key player with whom everyone could do business—in this case the business of getting Johnson elected.

Nevertheless, it was early September before Johnson instructed O'Brien to arrange a series of some twenty-one confidential regional meetings, in which he, Johnson, could take the measure of the political situation in every state.

Until then Johnson had done, as Kenny put it, "almost nothing about the campaign." Then suddenly he jumped in, complaining to Larry and Kenny that he "felt out of touch," and assigned O'Brien to be "the presidential eyes and ears on the road."

O'Brien was to talk politics to a dozen or so top leaders in every state. In these mostly behind-the-scenes meetings held state by state, O'Brien "ruthlessly laid out" the Johnson strategy. After six weeks of meetings, he finally locked himself in his hotel room where he wrote a voluminous confidential report for the president, which was sent by Western Union to the White House the instant it was finished.

For Johnson, who admitted he had never had the benefit of "such professional political help," the O'Brien reports became "The Word." Johnson ordered their recommendations carved up and distributed among the White House staff and over at the Democratic National Committee.

"For Johnson," Kenny explained, "such professional political insight and skill on a campaign was completely new. For us, John Kennedy had expected this level of professionalism from his first campaign for Senate in 1952. Larry O'Brien was the best of the best, so Johnson understood he was benefitting from one of the best minds in the political business."

Johnson ordered his special assistant Walter Jenkins, Kenny, and staff at the Democratic National Committee to follow through on each and every recommendation by O'Brien. Johnson was so impressed with O'Brien, he eventually ordered

Walter Jenkins to provide him with a traveling staff, including one secretary, one assistant, and the ability to confidentially telephone in his weekly reports to the White House stenographers to have them immediately type up the reports for the president's eyes only.

The O'Brien report gave Johnson "something he had never had before: a political road map of the United States, each area filled in with facts and figures," as O'Brien explained it later. "Even if the president's organization remained chaotic, as it had in 1960, his political intelligence was the best I could give him."

"Larry O'Brien and pollster Oliver Quayle were at that time the best in the political business," Kenny said. "No matter how disorganized or even disheveled Johnson's campaign was and perhaps remained through the fall of 1964, his political intelligence from O'Brien and the polls from Quayle were the best and right on target. Even with a chaotic campaign, there was no question this data put Johnson in a very strong position. Goldwater had nobody of this caliber on his team."

Kenny confirmed that Johnson was delighted. "The president said to me that he was 'as impressed with O'Brien as a man can be of his political skills. The man is a genius.'"

Kenny was relieved, admittedly for himself, in that O'Brien was stepping into the gap as the point person to Johnson, taking some of the pressure off Kenny and by connection Bobby.

"Look," Kenny said, "Johnson did not have any of the uneasiness with Larry that he had with me, and certainly he had no relationship with Bobby by now. Larry was really brilliant at this key moment in our political life and I think that contribution has been somewhat overlooked. Johnson would have won anyway, but it was Larry's intelligence and skill that made sure he won by the decisive numbers that the president wanted and frankly needed for his own sense of success."

CHAPTER FIFTEEN

THE ANTI-CAMPAIGN

While Johnson appreciated O'Brien's political brilliance, he was taking no chances. Despite all the assurances that Goldwater was so politically extreme that Johnson could easily win, he was ever fretful and insecure when it came to his own political fate. Therefore, even with the positive poll results he had seen from Ollie Quayle, Johnson decided to take another unusual step. Johnson instituted and took personal charge of a group he named the "Anti-Campaign," a step Kenny said John Kennedy never would have taken.

According to Bob Novak, "No political operation in history was conducted with such secrecy. The Anti-Campaign was clandestine 'black propaganda' organized by a dozen brainy Washington-based Democrats, some in and some out of government. It had no chairman, kept no minutes, issued no statements, revealed no strategy. No word of the Anti-Campaign leaked out. It operated out of a small conference room on the second floor of the West Wing of the White House, almost directly above the president's Oval Office. The entire operation was conceived and watched over by Lyndon Johnson; it was his unique contribution to the presidential campaign."

The job of the so-called Anti-Campaign group was, as Kenny understood from Johnson, to "embarrass the Republicans, get under Barry Goldwater's skin, thereby achieving Johnson's overall goal as outlined by O'Brien of winning by the biggest possible margin." Kenny thought the entire thing mad.

"John Kennedy would never have conducted such an operation," Kenny told Johnson with disgust. "He believed in winning by inspiration, not dirty politics."

But Johnson was insistent. If Kenny didn't want to participate that was fine, but he had to keep his mouth shut.

"I told nobody about this," Kenny said later, "except Bobby, who thought it was so nuts that at first he thought I was making it up."

"It sounds like something out of a movie," Bobby exclaimed in disbelief.

But this was no movie. This group of serious men were some of the most prominent and powerful players both in and out of government. Novak later reported these men were "prominent, security-conscious, well-versed in the propaganda of politics." They included:

> Myer Feldmen, the president's Special Counsel; Adam Yarmolinsky, back at the Defense Department after his purge from the War on Poverty; Daniel Patrick Moynihan, an Assistant Secretary of Labor; Leonard Marks, an old friend of Johnson and an attorney who specialized in communications law; Tyler Abel, Assistant Postmaster General and husband of Mrs. Johnson's social secretary; James Sundquist, an Assistant Secretary of Agriculture and former Truman speechwriter; Herman Bookbinder, a former labor lobbyist and lieutenant to Hubert Humphrey; D. B.

Hardemann, confidential assistant to the late speaker Sam Rayburn; Myer Rashish, an expert on international trade. And then there were three prominent Washington lawyers: Tom Finney, fresh from his work on the Atlantic City convention; John Sharon, a former Adlai Stevenson campaign aide and, like Finney, a member of Clark Clifford's law firm; and Robert Martin, who had worked for Johnson's campaign in 1960.

The group undertook a number of efforts, most prominent and effective of which included taking an editorial published by prominent theologian Reinhold Niebuhr, which included a "scathing editorial against Barry Goldwater as a man not to be entrusted with the presidency."

These various articles placed in various publications would eventually make their way into larger circulation, but Johnson's Anti-Campaign staff got hold of them, duplicated them by the hundreds, and using existing Democratic political contacts blasted them out to churches and other appropriate groups within days. They saturated the ground, forcing Goldwater to have to constantly respond to these articles and editorials.

Another tactic was more in the realm of "black politics," as Kenny called it. It was a tactic that Kenny said "John Kennedy might have appreciated, but would never have felt the need to use."

The Anti-Campaign group would get a list of all Goldwater's scheduled speaking engagements, then they would schedule an event at the same location an hour before the speech and another one right after Goldwater spoke, busing in supporters to overwhelm the Goldwater audience. These speeches were often given by Democrats or whenever possible Republicans who had come out against Goldwater.

As Bob Novak put it, "Goldwater would be bracketed by the opposition. An impression of feverish anti-Goldwater activity would be given on the very day of his appearance. It was designed to be picked up by the media and generate stories of the Goldwater campaign being in trouble."

Bob Novak reported that another tactic was to "make generous use of the letters columns of local newspapers. The Anti-Campaign group would find a local well-known Republican businessman known to be backing Johnson to write an anti-Goldwater piece to the local paper. Then they would manufacture many letters from local people backing the editorial." All this was carefully scheduled to happen on the day Goldwater's campaign swept into town.

But for Johnson, who was worried about not winning by a large enough landslide, such tactics needed reinforcements. Thus he came up with his own plan, which he dubbed "frontlash."

"This frontlash strategy was Lyndon Johnson's own contribution to the vocabulary of 1964 and was a key element of his so-called Anti-Campaign," said Novak.

Johnson had examined Ollie Quayle's poll for evidence of the fearful backlash—Democratic voters North and South defecting to Goldwater because of resentment against what the press had dubbed the "Negro Revolution."

But as he examined the poll numbers Johnson was surprised. "Instead, he found a majority of Republican voters were defecting to Johnson rather than voting for Goldwater and so he [Johnson] promptly dubbed it frontlash."

According to the evidence, Novak said Quayle's polls showed that the "Negrophobic character of the backlash was clear enough, the roots of the frontlash seemed to grow out of Republican distrust of Goldwater as well as Johnson's ability to reach across the political divide and build a consensus."

Johnson was determined to use "frontlash" as best he could to, as he put it, "bury Goldwater and make him appear so extreme he frightened the voters."

Key to the campaign strategy was, as Johnson explained it, "hacking away at Goldwater's character and continuing to enlarge his political consensus and deepening the political divide between those few who supported Goldwater and the vast majority who will vote for me."

Kenny said later that he found all these outsiders and various groups, names, and strategies chaotic and confusing. However, he admitted he "could not argue with the story that Ollie Quayle's polls were telling."

That said, he found the "sprawling, disorganized Johnson campaign frustrating." When he had a moment to bring Bobby up to speed about it, Bobby admitted he shared Kenny's confusion.

"How can you tell who is doing what?" Bobby asked.

Kenny admitted he had no idea and was beginning to realize such "campaign by chaos," as Kenny dubbed it, was actually Johnson's strategy. "I think he knows exactly what is going on, where and with whom, but I think he is the only one who does and maybe that is the point."

Bobby, who was struggling with his own campaign in New York, professed to have no idea.

"All I can say," Bobby said to Kenny, "is this gives you more time to help me." This was exactly what Kenny did, while still keeping his hand in the Johnson campaign as needed, and at the White House. But increasingly he was more focused on Bobby than Johnson.

"Rightly or not," Kenny confessed, "government by chaos is not how I operate and it was not how John Kennedy would ever operate. I found it very frustrating, but it seemed to be, at least for the political moment, effective. How long such a strategy could last is anybody's guess. My own view, and Bobby was in complete agreement with me on this: in the long run you cannot successfully govern by chaos."

That may be true, but in the meantime, the chaotic and now sprawling Johnson campaign lurched forward with or without Kenny's approval. Johnson had his own style and increasingly, as time went on and his confidence in himself as president grew, he was making decisions that Kenny would only learn about later, sometimes only from his reporter pals on the White House beat.

"There was no question that he understood my disapproval of some of this approach, so often I was the odd man out within the Johnson inner circle. This only increased my determination to stay only until the end of the year," Kenny recalled.

The next step was to put together what Johnson called the National Independent Committee for Johnson and Humphrey. The committee was put together by James Rowe, a longtime pal of Johnson and Kenny, who was chairman of the Johnson campaign. A hard-nosed political operative who Kenny liked, Rowe was devoted to Johnson in much the way Kenny had been devoted to John Kennedy.

The committee was announced from the Rose Garden at the White House on September 3 and its job was to, as Johnson explained it, "create a political consensus around the Johnson campaign, making him the candidate for all Americans." This was the front door strategy, allowing the "black politics" and the Anti-Campaign to do the "tough stuff," as Johnson said to Kenny, "just behind the scenes."

Bob Novak wrote that "the list of members of this new Committee read like a *Who's Who* of Eastern big business, men and titles linked to the Republican Party of Thomas E. Dewey and Dwight D. Eisenhower, but now cast adrift by the nomination of Barry Goldwater and now wondrously attached to the Johnson-Humphrey standard. The list of attendees featured names such as Henry Ford II of Ford Motor Company; Marion B. Folsom and Robert Anderson from the Eisenhower cabinet; Thomas S. Lamont and ex-Republican kingmaker Sidney J. Weinberg of Wall Street."

"The list," Novak reported, "would be a prestigious collector's item for any Democratic presidential nominee to carry into a national campaign.

"During his announcement of the committee held in the cabinet room, Johnson spelled out his philosophy. It was taken straight out of frontlash and watered down in such a manner to make it as easy as possible for these Republican businessmen to turn their backs on the Republican party to support Johnson."

Kenny was there that day, off to the side, and while he had not played a major role in the creation of the committee, he could not argue with Johnson's clear statement of its mission. Johnson began awkwardly enough, but got quickly to the point:

> I did not, I do not, and I shall never seek to be a labor president, or a business president, a president for liberals or a president for conservatives, a president for the North or a president for the South—but only a president for all the people.

Evans and Novak reported that Johnson's "frontlash politics exploited the staid Republican businessman's fear of Goldwater as an undependable radical politician. The result was an unprecedented flood of large contributions for the Johnson campaign, which with Johnson's Texas money opened up financial resources never before available to a Democratic nominee."

"We were swimming in money," reported Kenny's sister, Justine, who still worked at the Democratic National Committee.

For the voter—the everyday voter whom Johnson wanted to reach—the money was used to put forth the message of this frontlash strategy in the most frightening terms possible. The idea was to deepen the view many Americans had that Goldwater was extreme, right wing, out of control, and could not be trusted. This message was carried out to the voters by television and radio commercial, but it was a page right out of Johnson's frontlash strategy. These commercials created by the advertising firm of Doyle Dane Bernbach, who had never done politics but were at the time considered a top firm on Madison Avenue. Their campaign would have a devastating effect on the Goldwater campaign and national politics from that point forward. The television commercials would become, for better or worse, classics in the history of political campaigns.

The idea behind the commercials was, as Novak and Evans reported at the time, "to terrify the voters with the mere thought of Barry Goldwater in the White House. They were not about what Johnson could do for the country, but rather what Goldwater might do to the country."

One of the spots included the now famous shot of a little girl pulling petals from a daisy, each petal fluttering to the ground with what Evans and Novak described at the time as a voice-over in which a "gloom-laden voice recited the countdown for firing intercontinental ballistic missile."

The other spot contained a hand that looked like Barry Goldwater's hand reaching for the nuclear button. Another controversial television ad showed a Social Security card being torn in two; the voice-over sounded suspiciously like Barry Goldwater. The ad was classic frontlash propaganda, designed to stoke fear among the elderly that Goldwater was a threat to their Social Security.

Kenny was appalled at the pieces and told Johnson as much. During a dinner in New York with Bobby to discuss Bobby's Senate campaign, Bobby too complained. He said he thought "the commercials went too far."

Bobby went on to complain to Kenny that he was getting "lots of criticism and complaints about the spots while on the campaign trail. They make us all look bad."

Kenny agreed, but reminded Bobby that his influence with Johnson these days was "not terribly strong. Maybe you should call him," Kenny suggested jokingly.

Bobby made a face at Kenny and said, "That's a great idea. If I complain he will double the running time of the commercials." Kenny laughed, but admitted that he didn't completely disagree. "I don't think he cares too much about what we think just now," he said.

But Bobby and Kenny were not the only ones uncomfortable with what Larry O'Brien called this "dark strategy." On a political fact-finding trip through Cleveland, O'Brien was bombarded with complaints.

After a few calls back and forth between Larry, Bobby, and Kenny, O'Brien took his complaints straight to the White House. He told Johnson that he had heard so much criticism that he strongly recommended killing at least the daisy spot, if not both.

O'Brien's recommendations were immediately followed. Both ads were pulled the next day. The Madison Avenue firm continued to serve the campaign, but with a slightly turned down approach.

What Kenny found most fascinating about Johnson's approach to his campaign was his all-in involvement behind the scenes. Yet in public he professed to have little or no interest.

Kenny said, "John Kennedy loved a good campaign. He was unabashed in his enthusiasm and excitement. He jumped in 100 percent and never looked back. Johnson seemed to at once want to win and win by enormous margins and yet at the same moment appear disinterested."

Kenny said Johnson told him once that September, "I don't want to look overly interested just in case I don't win. Something happens and I don't win by the big margins. I want to appear as if I didn't care one way or the other."

"I was just puzzled," Kenny admitted. "John Kennedy never thought he would lose. He just assumed he would work hard enough and was smart enough to win. That is why the few times he did lose, say in 1956, and during the first Cuba crisis, it was a real shock to him. He just never had an insecure moment in his political life. But Johnson, despite all he had done in his career and his presidency to this moment, was a bundle of insecurities."

Johnson went so far as to hold a press conference on September 5 at the White House disavowing any interest in the campaign and professing to be surprised at all the work being done on his behalf. When pressed again and again by skeptical reporters, Johnson replied with a classic Johnsonian dodge:

We have a job to do here and we are going to try to do that first. When, as, and if we can, we will make appearances as we think we can without neglecting the interests of the nation. . . . But just where I will be at some certain day in October I can't determine and I don't want to announce because then you will have me canceling and adjusting my plans, things of that kind. That makes more of a story than my appearance would make.

Reporters were having none of it. Rollie Evans and Bob Novak reported at the time that "Johnson would have us believe that it was, then, to be a campaign that started with the president's insistence that it was no campaign at all."

For example, two days before he went to Detroit to open the Democratic campaign with the traditional Labor Day appearance at Cadillac Square, Johnson was asked what kind of speech he had in mind.

The president's reply was received with great amusement by the traveling press:

> We never characterize any speech. The president of the United States is not in the business of applying labels and making speculations on matters of this kind. You will have copies of the speech and if you want to indulge in that, it is all right. You can say it is constructive, progressive, prudent, or radical; it is political or nonpolitical; whatever you want to say about it. I don't care.

With this announcement of no announcement, the Johnson campaign was fully under way. On September 28 at the portico of the *Hartford Times*, Johnson finally set the tone for the campaign in what reporters called his "own clear, unadorned style":

> There is a time for party and there is a place for partisanship. But there are times in the history of a nation when higher values matter more than party, and there are greater issues than partisanship.
>
> All that America is, and all you want America to be is challenged today by those who stand on the fringe. Against such a choice as this, responsible people have only one course of conscience, and that is to choose their country's interest over all other interests. I believe that this choice that you will make come this November.

This simple statement, written not by Johnson's army of speechwriters, but rather by Johnson himself, came from the heart. And with it, in all its simplicity, the campaign was full steam ahead.

Kenny, in his office at the DNC, got a call from Bobby.

"Finally!" Bobby said. "But it was good," he said of Johnson's statement. "Who wrote it?"

Kenny laughed. "He did. It came right from the heart."

Evans and Novak reported that a few days later, Johnson, on a roll from a wildly successful swing through John Kennedy's old hometown of Boston and New England, continued his theme of portraying himself as a rational, prudent consensus builder facing off against a "warmongering Barry Goldwater."

During one press event, Johnson spoke from the heart:

> You don't get peace by rattling your rockets. You don't get peace by threatening to drop bombs. You must have strength, and you must always keep your guard up, but you must always have your hand out and be willing to go any-where, talk to anybody, listen to anything they have to say, do anything that is honorable, in order to avoid pulling that trigger, mashing that button that will blow up the world.

As he finished the last line, he used his hand to mimic the action of pressing that nuclear button. "We can do better," he said, calling his audience to his side. The response was positive and immediate.

Back in Washington, Kenny was pleased. Johnson seemed to be hitting his stride and while Bobby was still in a battle, each day he grew a bit better as a candidate. "Bobby was a terrible candidate compared to his brother," Kenny recalled. "But he was getting better each day; so I felt we would win the White House by the numbers Larry had hoped for, and

Bobby would finish strong and end up in the Senate. None of us expected to be here, but we were here now and everyone was pulling towards the next step."

CHAPTER SIXTEEN
VICTORY

As disorganized as the Johnson campaign was by Kennedy campaign standards, Johnson was being greeted by enormous crowds who seemed enthusiastic and supportive of the new president.

"Yet," reported Rowland Evans and Bob Novak, "for all his high success on the campaign trail, however, the president sometimes grew gloomy—not because he feared defeat but because he doubted the depth of people's affection for him."

To two old friends, J. W. Fulbright and Dean Acheson, the president separately and sadly complained in mid-October that, notwithstanding his own triumphant campaign tours, "too many people seemed to be backing him only because of Goldwater's unacceptability."

One evening, Johnson called Kenny at the Democratic National Committee and asked him to come by for a drink and a chat. Kenny had seen the crowds as they moved through October, and he had to admit that while this was not the campaign he would have run, and despite all the problems, Johnson was well ahead in Ollie Quayle's polls. He seemed to have little to fear and

Kenny even thought there was "a better than ever chance he would make Warren Harding's 64 percentage mark. I thought he would be happy. He should have been. I assumed he wanted to discuss the campaign closing in towards November or maybe even ask some questions about Bobby's campaign, but I was surprised to find him down and very gloomy."

Johnson began by telling Kenny what he had been telling friends in private for weeks, that he was pleased by the crowds and the poll numbers, but he worried that it was not enough. Kenny sipped his drink and listened, which was what he often did with Johnson.

"I sometimes felt he just needed a sounding board. Somebody he could let off steam to about whatever was bothering him, realizing that it would go no further. But this time I was puzzled. When he finished we sat in silence for a moment sipping our drinks," Kenny recalled. "I was trying to find the best way to word what I had to say.

"'Mr. President,' I said, 'According to Larry, he feels you will make the goal of 64 percent. That is a substantial victory that any candidate would be delighted to receive.'"

Johnson sat for a moment before leaning in to Kenny.

"I understand that, but the question is are these people voting for me, Lyndon Johnson, or just against Barry Goldwater? I didn't want it this way. You know that, but I also don't want to be elected because I am just seen as the 'lesser of two evils.'" He leaned forward and seemed to be searching Kenny's face for answers, maybe reassurance. But Kenny was never a faker and was not going to start now.

"Look, Mr. President," Kenny said, "who the hell cares? You will win by huge numbers when you make the presidency your own; people will learn to appreciate you for the things you accomplish for them and the country."

Kenny told Bobby later he could see almost immediately Johnson was disappointed.

"I could see this was not the answer he was looking for from me," Kenny said to Bobby. "I am not sure what else I could say. He is not your brother, after all. That said, he should be delighted with the numbers that it looks like he will win by. But you know your brother would never have had such doubts. He would take the win, then use his success to win over those voters who were in doubt."

Bobby laughed. "Well, Kenny, I hope you didn't say that to him! I have no tact at all, but even I wouldn't say that to him."

The truth was that Johnson was not entirely wrong in his view that people were voting for him in such large numbers because they saw him as the "lesser of two evils." Rowland Evans and Bob Novak reported in their column a month or so after the election, when all the numbers had been counted, that "this lesser of two evils had some basis in fact, polls indicated after the election when the total vote was found to be 1.2 percent less than the 1960 vote as a proportion of the total number of eligibles."

Johnson showed the piece to Kenny almost with a sense of triumph.

"I told you," he growled at Kenny.

Kenny, who by then was preparing to leave the White House but had yet to make it official, simply shook his head.

"You won, Mr. President," Kenny reminded him. "My father was a football coach. Football is like politics: a win is a win."

Johnson walked off without saying a word.

Kenny may have been content to take a win any way he could, but Johnson was not. At dinner one night in October, Johnson pressed his longtime friends J. William Fulbright and Dean Acheson on the subject. He wanted to know whether or not they felt he should change his image.

"I want them to feel for me as they did for John Kennedy," he insisted. The two friends tried to reassure the gloomy president.

First, Fulbright and Acheson told him, he was . . . correct in thinking himself not the best loved president in history; second that it did not make the slightest difference because *great* presidents were often not *greatly* loved presidents.

Lyndon Johnson was not pleased with their answer. Bob Novak said later, "Lyndon Johnson, whose quest for power had always been laced with an appetite for the public's affection, was not impressed."

All of these conversations and the president's growing gloominess led to a request being sent to Kennedy and Johnson friend John Kenneth Galbraith. Galbraith, whose intellectualism especially impressed Johnson, was pressed by Fulbright, Acheson, and Larry O'Brien to write a pamphlet making the case for Lyndon Johnson's presidency. "The goal," Larry explained to Kenny, "was to put the president in a more positive light."

Galbraith wrote what can only be described as an unemotional, closely reasoned argument:

> Johnson deserves an overwhelming vote for President not because Goldwater was the only other choice, but because quite simply no one measures up better in our time. It is not enough that we elect President Johnson. We must elect him with a sense of satisfaction in our opportunity and warm pride in our man.

"John Kennedy didn't need a pamphlet to tell him that he was the right man for the job," Kenny had complained to Larry.

"No, he didn't," Larry agreed. "But it is a new time and a new president, Kenny."

Kenny told his wife later that he knew Larry was correct.

"Johnson needs his own people," Kenny admitted to her. "I am not the fellow he needs right now."

She wanted to disagree, but didn't know how.

For the Goldwater campaign, Goldwater's most senior advisors understood Johnson's overwhelming strength and, in truth, saw little potential for a major political upset. If it was going to happen, they would need to find a chink in the Johnson armor using what they called the "morality issue."

Evans and Novak reported that a "vague, unfavorable image of the president—based partly on emotion, partly on his reputation as a Texas wheeler dealer not unwilling to cut a corner here or there—had taken hold in the country."

"As is always with these political moods," Kenny said, "some was based simply in innuendo . . . along with the cold hard facts that Johnson had amassed a personal fortune since being in the Senate and the White House as president and vice president. This was money he had amassed since being in power and it was quite apart from his wife's money." Of course, there was nothing particularly unusual about that at the time, but the Republicans felt it was their only real way to damage Johnson.

Their first hope was that Johnson's old protégé, Bobby Baker, whose scandal was now erupting in the Senate Rules Committee, would somehow implicate Johnson. Johnson would fume about the Baker hearings on a regular basis to Kenny, saying, not incorrectly, that the hearings had become "political in nature." At other, darker moments, he would remind Kenny that it was "your pal Bobby Kennedy that started this entire mess."

Kenny recalled, "I would remind the president that the Baker problem happened while John Kennedy was in the White

House and Bobby was attorney general. Surely Bobby would never have deliberately damaged his brother's administration."

Johnson would shrug it off.

"He knew I was correct, but he was understandably concerned. We were very close to the election at this point and the Republican National Committee was trying to dig up dirt at every turn."

While the Baker scandal continued to generate headlines, it never touched Johnson directly; instead the public viewed it more as a stain on Congress, despite the Goldwater's campaign to paint a different picture. But Johnson would not be so lucky with the fate of longtime aide Walter Jenkins. Jenkins had been with Johnson for nearly twenty-five years. His wife was very close to Lady Bird and he was deeply loyal. His daughter and Linda Johnson were best friends.

Kenny had gotten to known Jenkins in the 1960 campaign. "He was a tremendous fellow," Kenny said. "Sharp, smart, classy, and tough-minded. He was very loyal to Johnson. Just a great all-around guy whom I turned to often as a conduit between Johnson and myself. Both Bobby and I felt he could be trusted completely."

Johnson felt much the same as Kenny until political and personal disaster struck. On October 7, according to reports at the time, White House Special Assistant Walter Jenkins was arrested along with another man—in the men's room of the YMCA, one block west of the White House on G Street, for "disorderly conduct."

Rumors quickly ran through Washington that this was the tip of some larger scandal in the Johnson White House. The Republican National Committee jumped in with both feet, helping to spread rumors, many of which were fiction, but all of which were damaging to Walter Jenkins's family and to the Johnson White House. Abe Fortas and Clark Clifford, finally realizing that this was only escalating thanks to the RNC's rumor mills, jumped in to try to stop the press from publishing the story. They went personally to each editor but were turned away. United Press International was the first wire service to run a major story above the fold and it hit all across the country.

Walter Jenkins had loyally and faithfully served Johnson for twenty-five years. "He was exhausted beyond belief," Kenny said. "It was a stupid mistake made ten times worse by the lies and fictions put out by the Republican National Committee, who saw this as a way to injure Johnson, and they had no regard for the damage they were doing to Walter's family."

Johnson, who was out on the road campaigning, said nothing. He never mentioned Jenkins, the scandal or his aide of twenty-five years. Not once. It fell to Mrs. Johnson, who told friends she was "heartsick over the tragedy." She immediately issued a strong statement in sympathy for Jenkins and his family. Johnson, campaigning in New York, continued to say nothing despite pleas from his wife, aides, and friends that he say something—anything. Johnson remained silent.

"Johnson was torn," Kenny explained, "by his friendship and loyalty to Walter, and the political reality that the election was only three weeks away. In fairness, I talked to Walter and he was not upset with Johnson. He understood more than anybody the difficult position the president was now facing. He was heartsick. We all were. Even Bobby with his own campaign called me and asked if there was anything he could do to help Walter's family. I told him to stay out of it. I was afraid at this precarious moment even a well-meaning gesture might be misinterpreted by the president."

Rowland Evans and Bob Novak later reported: "In those dark hours on October 14, a wave of fear swept through the White House that this could be the happening that would change the course of history. Jenkins had been privy to every piece of classified intelligence in the White House. Was it possible that he had been subject to blackmail, that the incident of October 7, or perhaps previous incidents, had been exploited by enemies of the United States? Within hours and to the roar of approval from Republican audiences, Goldwater began talking about Johnson's 'curious crew' at the White House."

As the dark political waters swirled around the White House, Johnson, reported Bob Novak, "resolved the conflict between friendship and the election by coming down on the side of the election." He did not speak directly to Walter Jenkins but ordered longtime friend Abe Fortas to get Jenkins's formal resignation, and he called J. Edgar Hoover over at the FBI. He instructed Hoover to initiate a full investigation into Walter Jenkins and issue a full report. The FBI did just that. A report finally issued at the end of October indicated that there was no evidence of any other incidents or that Jenkins had compromised the security of the United States.

Johnson's quick and decisive action seemed to have the necessary effect and O'Brien and Quayle's polls showed that the public was largely satisfied with the actions Johnson had taken. The entire tragic story was suddenly overshadowed by news from Moscow that John Kennedy's nemesis Nikita Khrushchev had been deposed. The public was now much more worried about the Soviet Union than Walter Jenkins.

"Efforts by the Goldwater campaign to use this personal tragedy as a symbol of decadence in the Johnson administration had failed," reported Bob Novak. The issue had nearly been forgotten until a few weeks later. Johnson, giving a speech in San Diego, inexplicably said that the Eisenhower administration had also had problems with "sexual deviants." The comment sent the press scrambling, but it turned out that the young man in question had only applied for a job with

Eisenhower and not actually received one before he got in trouble.

Kenny said, "Mentioning it again was a foolish and stupid thing to do. I told the president as much. By raising it he risked starting the story up all over again. I said to him, it was a cheap shot. He shook his head at me. He was angry and he was tired. Maybe too tired to argue? I am not sure he even knew why he had said it himself. The entire story was just a tragedy. But for Johnson it could have been a real political disaster, but it wasn't—thank God."

Nothing came of the incident. As Sander Vanocur of NBC news reported at the time, "It would seem nothing could help save Goldwater and nothing can hurt Lyndon Johnson in 1964."

Election eve found Johnson in Austin, Texas, preparing for one of the most important days of his life.

The next day Rowland Evans and Bob Novak reported the victory was sweet for President Johnson. They wrote that "Goldwater carried a mere 60 congressional districts out of 435, running far behind his party. Johnson ran far ahead in his, expanding the Democrats' majorities in the Senate by 2 seats and in the House by 37, to a point not exceeded since the 1936 election . . . he captured slightly over 61 percent of the presidential votes, and 486 electoral votes, the highest since Roosevelt's 1936 sweep . . . but Johnson had failed to equal Roosevelt's 63 percent in 1936 and Harding's 64 percent in 1920 . . . but behind the statistics was a revolution in American politics."

Kenny spent the election in New York with Bobby. He should have been either at the Washington headquarters of the Johnson campaign or in Austin, but he wasn't. He told Sandy Vanocur later that the president had not asked him to join him in Austin, and nobody would miss him in Washington.

Sandy said later, "I think he was relieved. He was happy Johnson won in his own right, but it was still painful and bittersweet for both Kenny and Bobby." At some level Johnson seemed to understand. He made a special effort to talk with Kenny that night, and to thank him. "This has not been an easy year for any of us," he said. "But we did it together."

Ironically, the troubled political waters in Texas that had, in part, brought John Kennedy to Dallas in November 1963 had finally begun to calm. As it turned out, the feuding Democrats were all winners. Kenny said, "Johnson ran behind Connally, but ahead of Senator Ralph Yarborough . . . Having skillfully headed off a primary fight by Joe Kilgore against Yarborough, Johnson now campaigned hard for his old enemy in the last hours of the campaign." Johnson gave a speech in favor of Yarborough in Houston, Texas on November 2:

> I don't know what is going to happen tomorrow but I know what I am going to do. I am going to get up early and I am going down to Johnson City, Texas, courthouse and I am going to put a vote in for Ralph Yarborough and I am not going to do it just because I like him or because he is a friend. I am going to do it because I think he has loyally and effectively worked for the Democratic program, for all people, and I want to be president of all the people.

Later that day, Johnson went to his ranch to await the results. Despite all the chaos of the campaign, a campaign that, as Evans and Novak said, "had no central management and no coordination, with the right hand not knowing what the left hand was doing . . . and despite Johnson's own personal insecurities and doubts . . . the campaign was a complete success . . . yet this campaign which may have changed no more than a handful of votes, changed Lyndon Johnson completely."

"He may not be loved in Washington and by the egg-heads and the stylish intellectuals," said Bob Novak, "but he had proved to himself that he could be loved and had been accepted by the masses in the North. Acceptance of this sol-itary fact by Johnson himself—his last unmet goal—was the consummation of his power as a politician."

"He finally felt he had done it on his own," Kenny said. "He had finally reached the pinnacle of power and he had done it his own way. With that I hoped he could put the doubts he had about himself and the suspicion about others behind and finally trust in his own skill and prowess as a politician. He had all the gifts but self-confidence. Now, I felt he would have that conquered as well. At least I hoped so for him and the country."

Late on election night, Lyndon Johnson, the newly elected president, left the Driskill Hotel in Austin where he had been staying to watch the election results. Johnson and his entou-rage drove over in the presidential limo to the Civic Center to give his acceptance speech. But instead of euphoria and enjoy-ing the sense of accomplishment, Johnson seemed to inexpli-cably grow angry as they headed over. His mood was triggered when he heard news reports on the radio announcing the president was headed over to the Civic Center. It was a minor mistake on the part of the press office, since Johnson had not authorized any statement be released yet. But the tension of the last year seemed to explode in this moment. The president had "authorized no such announcement," he growled at assis-tant press secretary Malcom Kilduff (the same Mac Kilduff whom Kenny had fired just before the fateful trip to Dallas in November 1963). Johnson exploded in a moment of anger, which was strange given his success at the moment.

But, after taking a few minutes to gather himself, to the astonishment of all gathered, Johnson approached Kilduff and apologized for losing his cool that way. "I was wrong, Mac. I am sorry," Johnson said. "Guess it was just the tension of the moment." Governor Connally, Johnson's longtime friend, who was with Johnson backstage, was astonished, saying to Kilduff, "It was the first time in all these years I've ever heard him make an apology."

As Rowland Evans and Bob Novak reported, "On November 3, 1964, Lyndon Johnson, his power consolidated, stood ready to build his great society—and a consensus America."

In January, columnist James Reston wrote:

Washington is now a little girl settling down with her old boyfriend. The mad and wonderful infatuation with the handsome stranger from Boston is over—somehow she always knew it wouldn't last—so she is adjusting to reality. Everything is less romantic and more practical, part regret, part relief; beer instead of champagne; not fancy but plain; and in many ways more natural and hopefully more durable. This may not be the best, most attractive quality of the new administration, but it works. . . . The lovers of style are not too happy with the new Administration, but the lovers of substance are not complaining.

While Lyndon Johnson geared up the Great Society, his first battle was to be civil rights. Kenny had drinks with Bobby in New York and said what they both knew to be true: "Now that you are safely in the Senate with Teddy, time for me to go home." Bobby nodded. They sat quietly for a moment.

Finally, Bobby said, "I think my brother would say we did the right things this past year, now it is time to move forward and move on."

Kenny nodded in agreement.

Indeed, it was time to move on. The years of John F.

Kennedy and Camelot had come to an end; they would now move from reality to mythology. Lyndon Johnson would forge ahead, finally a president in his own right, and he had won by following his own unique style. If Johnson thought having Bobby Kennedy in the Senate would allow him to finally relax in his fear that Bobby remained in many people's eyes the president in waiting, he was very much mistaken. The epic battles with his nemesis were far from over. But all this was in the future. For now, Kenny, Bobby, Larry, and for that matter Johnson himself had survived a difficult year. Like the country itself, they had come out stronger and perhaps better equipped for the next chapter. But this time it would be Lyndon Johnson and his Great Society that would change the fabric of American society forever.

CHAPTER SEVENTEEN
ON THEIR OWN

"The truth was that Lyndon Johnson made many mistakes that John Kennedy would never have made. That said, Barry Goldwater was such a pushover and so far out of the mainstream of even the Republican Party that Johnson's mistakes never hurt him," Kenny said later. He went on:

> It was a relief to see Lyndon Johnson safely elected on his own to the White House and taking over the presidency . . . with a solid feeling of security after the unhappy months of trying to fill out the remainder of John Kennedy's unfinished term—and work uncomfortably with Kennedy's cabinet and Kennedy's White House staff. He had wanted to be a good president when he was serving in the office as a stand-in for his dead predecessor, but he was always uncomfortably aware that most of the Kennedy-appointed people around him, particularly the Eastern Ivy Leaguers from the New Frontier administration, were cool towards him and regarded his presence in the White House as simply an unhappy accident. He was striving to do his best under unpleasant circumstances, and the situation was a hard one.

President Johnson and I always had a pleasant relationship during the four years that I worked in the White House. There were times of strain, mostly because of my friendship with Bobby. But for the most part he understood that and always tried to be respectful. When we argued over differences in political opinions, we never exchanged a harsh word nor did he ever engage in any personal attacks. He was always direct with me, and I always tried to do the same with him. I reminded him often during the 1964 campaign that I was planning to resign from his staff and move back to Boston and run for governor after the election, but he did not take me seriously. "No man willingly walks out of the White House," he would say to me.

Along with Dave Powers, Larry O'Brien, and the other remaining Kennedy Irishmen on the White House staff, I submitted to Johnson a letter of resignation to be effective at the end of the year, 1964. He ignored our letters. And after the election, [he] gave me several chores to keep me busy working for him. One of them was an assignment to recruit a new attorney general to replace Nicholas Katzenbach, Bobby's former deputy and close friend, who had been heading up the Department of Justice since Bobby resigned to run for the Senate in New York in August.

"Nick's a nice fellow," Johnson said, getting in a dig at Bobby. "But he's Bobby's friend, and we can't expect Bobby to keep on running the Justice Department now that he's in the Senate. Two jobs would be too much for even Bobby."

When I got home that night Bobby called with a list of reasons why Nick should be kept on as attorney general. I began to realize that I would never get away from Lyndon Johnson and out of the middle until I made the move on my own. I knew that would irritate Johnson. He disliked anybody leaving his staff voluntarily.

"Nobody leaves Lyndon Johnson unless Lyndon Johnson wants them to go," he would often say.

One day in January 1965, shortly before his inauguration, I told his assistants, Bill Moyers and Jack Valenti, to pass along the word that I was leaving whether my resignation was accepted or not. Moyers called me back and said the president would see me in his office in an hour. I found him standing at his desk with my letter of resignation in his hand. He was in a bad mood.

"So you're going to leave," he said.

I explained to him I wanted to go back to Boston. He said nothing at first. He did not ask me what I planned to do there nor did he wish me well, say good luck or even goodbye. He said only, "Well, it's all right with me, and when you leave take Powers with you. He's never worked for anybody around here except you and the Kennedys."

With that he turned his back on me. I turned and walked out, taking one last look to recall the day John Kennedy and I had first walked into the Oval Office. It seemed like a lifetime ago. Perhaps it was . . .

Lyndon Johnson never spoke to me again. That night Jackie called to see how I was and to tell me she believed I had done the right thing.

"It is time for us all to turn the page and move forward in life, no matter how difficult that may be. I think Jack would be proud of you," she said.

Somehow her words gave me some peace and clarity that with all that had happened, Bobby and I had done the best we could for John Kennedy, Lyndon Johnson, and most importantly, the country.

Perhaps the legislation that meant the most to Bobby and Kenny during this tumultuous year was the civil rights bill.

Though both men realized and assumed it would likely not get passed until after they both had left the administration, they were determined to do what they could to keep the issue front and center for Johnson.

They need not have worried. Johnson had actually introduced the first civil rights bill back when he was a senator. He did not necessarily need to be pushed by Bobby and Kenny to move ahead with the legislation.

According to Evans and Novak, "Johnson in his first hours as president was admittedly ambiguous about the Kennedy tax cut proposal, but there was no doubt where he stood on the civil rights bill. He made this clear to all the civil rights leaders—Dr. Martin Luther King, Roy Wilkins of the NAACP, Whitney Young of the Urban League, Joe Rauh of the ADA—in the first days after November 22. Summoning them to his office individually, he left no doubt he would at the very minimum stand with the bill approved on November 20 by the House Judiciary Committee."

The myth that Johnson had saved the failing Kennedy bill from a slow demise in Congress has, according to Novak, "little relationship to reality."

Novak insisted that the "great breakthrough in the civil rights legislative fight came a few days before President Kennedy's assassination when the White House, after weeks of wooing, finally obtained Rep. Charley Halleck's promise of support for the bill. The celebrated so-called 'thick bacon' breakfast between the new president and the house minority leader came after the fact of Halleck's decision to support Kennedy's civil rights legislation. Beyond that with Kennedy's death, there is little doubt that the bill ultimately would have passed late in 1964—after much debate, acrimony, and much horse trading—whether the president was Kennedy or Johnson—the bill would have passed."

Kenny insisted that he and Bobby both felt that much of the credit belonged to Larry O'Brien:

> This was before President Kennedy's death, but Larry had been working the House Judiciary Committee and Halleck very hard even before we left for Dallas. President Kennedy wanted that bill in 1964 and wanted to get it passed. He would like to have it passed before the election, but he understood that politically that might not be possible. It might be early 1965, but he was determined. He told Larry as much.
>
> During one meeting with Larry, shortly before Texas, the President said to him: "Larry, I want this bill. I would like to walk into the election with it under my arm." Larry then explained that while he thought a bill in late 1964 might be possible to get passed, the political price would be high.
>
> Larry told the president, "I think this could potentially cost us the Southern bloc, and could cost us the South for a generation at least."
>
> The president understood what Larry was saying, but pointed out that the cost of inaction would be much higher. I say all this to point out that it is a fallacy to say that Johnson saved the Kennedy civil rights bill. He continued to press the bill through Congress, but the bill was substantially unchanged from its original iteration under Kennedy. I know for a fact that President Kennedy was hoping for a bill by late 1964, if possible. Though he understood completely what Larry was telling him, which was this will not be easy and the cost will be high.
>
> The president said to me: "Kenny, this is a battle worth having . . ."

Kenny said that he laid all this out for Johnson in some of their first meetings after Kennedy's death:

I did not necessarily need to do this. Johnson did not need to be urged forward by anyone—his gut told him this was the right thing to do. This was an issue he was passionate about on his own. He had been one of the first to introduce a civil rights bill in the 1950s, and though the bill had failed, it left Johnson determined. It is my view the Kennedy bill would have passed anyway, but Johnson was able to use his substantial legislative skills with Congress to ensure its successful passage.

I remember saying to Bobby over drinks one night that President Kennedy would have been delighted to see Johnson in action forcing through this civil rights bill. God knows we could not get him to do any of that when he was vice president.

Bobby was quiet for a moment.

Then he said, "I guess it should not matter who gets the credit. The issue is important and it has all taken entirely too long, but I cannot help but believe that the bill's successful passage should be and will be a tribute to my brother."

According to Evans and Novak, "Even before the bill had passed the House on February 10 by a vote of 290 to 130, Johnson had laid down the no-compromise edict. In a private session in his office with Clarence Mitchell of the NAACP and Joe Rauh of ADA, Johnson pledged there would be no changes in the bill even if that required suspending all activity in the Senate for months."

In fact, when the House adopted the Fair Employment Practice Committee provisions on February 6, and the last vote on the bill was there, Johnson immediately acted. Without a moment to waste, he picked up the telephone to Joe Rauh and said: "What are you fellows doing about the Senate?" Rauh told Kenny he had been delighted to get the call.

Johnson had made clear in the call that he wanted the

Senate to pass the bill, as Johnson said to Rauh, "intact and including FEPC. I understand that will mean redoubling our efforts and rounding up enough support to break the inevitable filibuster by the Southerners. No doubt about it."

According to Novak, "Simultaneously, Johnson told his Senate leaders, Mike Mansfield and Majority Whip Humphrey, that he was prepared to sacrifice all other legislation in the Senate if necessary to break the civil rights filibuster. Now fully emancipated from his Southern base, there was no need to trim his civil rights legislation to please Dixie."

"On the contrary," Johnson told them. "If I trimmed away as Kennedy probably would have to wedge the bill through the Senate, I will be excoriated by the civil rights movement, by organized labor, and by liberals. I cannot afford that. We've got to put the whole thing through in one piece."

Evans and Novak later reported, "On this issue Johnson's political imperatives as a Southern president foreclosed compromise, whereas Kennedy's would not have. But beyond that, Johnson was now functioning from his new presidential power base."

Johnson later told Kenny and Larry: "I am determined to get the whole bill through and exercise complete control of Congress with no thought of compromise."

Kenny admitted later that he was skeptical as to whether Johnson could pull that off. "I just did not see how he could hold Congress hostage like that and get the entire package passed. But Larry told me in this instance I was wrong. Larry turned out to be correct. A few nights later Larry and I had dinner. We discussed the legislation and Larry said to me, 'Look, Kenny, if he is willing to play tough and hold up everything else, we can do it.'"

As the bill passed, Rowland Evans said, "Almost incredibly, Johnson won the whole package with no compromise. The death of President Kennedy had robbed civil rights opposition of much of its sting. The emotional reaction to Dallas changed the climate of opinion, both in Congress and in the country, and intangibly brought about a far more sympathetic response to the Negro revolution."

The powerful Senator Richard Russell, now older and unwell, nevertheless organized his followers and Southern political legions to block the bill just as he had successfully done in 1960 and in 1962, when he had been successful in pushing for state literacy tests that effectively disenfranchised the black voters. But this time he had no luck.

Kenny explained it this way: "Russell was not well. He was tired, his followers were tired, and I think they simply didn't have the gusto for a fight with Lyndon Johnson at this time, given President Kennedy's death and the mood of the country along with Johnson's determination for full passage. My own view is, and Bobby agreed, that they just didn't have the stomach for the battle at this time."

Bob Novak reported it this way: "Once the president had ruled out the possibility of compromise and declared his intention to suspend all other Senate business to outwait the filibusters, the Southerners knew they were beaten."

"Nobody knew how to play the Senate game better than Lyndon Johnson," Mike Mansfield told Kenny. "They knew they were beaten."

On July 2, Johnson signed the bill, which was not vastly different than the House bill passed on February 10.

Johnson had shown that while he could be flexible and maneuver with Congress when necessary, if he felt strong enough about something, he could be both determined and uncompromising. The press later asked the tired Senator Richard Russell, if, in the end, the bill would be watered down and "made more palatable."

"No," Russell answered tiredly, "the way this fellow [Johnson], now president, is operating, he'll get the whole bill. Every last bit of it."

In the end, that was exactly what happened.

Bobby was there for the signing and he told Larry and Kenny later: "It meant a great deal. It was what the president [Kennedy] would have wanted. And yet, while I stood there, all I could think of was the lost possibilities and ask myself why this happened this way."

Kenny and Larry had no answers to a question they no doubt asked themselves often. But while they were wondering, the new president was moving full steam ahead.

"He's come into his own," Richard Russell said. And while that was true, this would prove to be only the start of Johnson's legislative success and the beginning of his push for his Great Society.

Though, increasingly, Kenny and Bobby would be watching from the outside of what was now clearly Lyndon Johnson's White House.

President Johnson would not be satisfied with the passage of the civil rights bill alone. While congressional leaders had hoped for an early adjournment during the election year of 1964, President Johnson was having none of it. He insisted that Congress stay in session until they had passed a myriad of bills, many of which had begun under Kennedy, but had become Johnson bills.

Bob Novak said, "Johnson kept their feet to the fire until October 3, he wanted bill after bill passed, including bills that had been written off as dead in 1963. The bill to provide federal aid for mass transit facilities was revived and passed. Many of Kennedy's bills for additional federal help to college students were passed. Although Kennedy had not planned an all-out drive in Congress for his anti-poverty programs until after the 1964 election, Johnson rushed a program to Congress and got it passed. This included the wheat price support bill, which had largely been stuck in committee."

This enormous legislative push would include a large contingent of Democratic congressmen from Southern and the Northern cities. A cotton bill was added to win Southern votes; a food stamp bill which included provisions to distribute food for the needy and poor was thrown in to bring along big cities in the North.

After much wrangling, and at the suggestion of Hubert Humphrey, the two bills were combined and on April 8 the wheat–food stamp bill came to a vote in the House, winning decisively by a margin Johnson elatedly called "a squeaker": 211 to 203. Johnson was thrilled. While O'Brien may have been his legislative liaison, the success was pure Johnson, who worked the phones till all hours, twisted arms, wooed, pushed, and pressed his former colleagues to the limit.

"The result and his success," Kenny said, "was pure Johnson and showed the difference between Johnson in the Senate and as vice-president. He was now president with all the power that entails, thus he was free to wield power in his own unorthodox style."

"You could not argue with the success," Kenny said to Bobby, "but certainly John Kennedy would have approached it differently."

Johnson's next big push was on Medicare and the key to that was Wilbur Mills. According to Kenny, John Kennedy had been working on Mills since 1961. "Their friendship had gotten stronger and stronger; I believe had John Kennedy lived, he would have supported a Medicare bill."

But Johnson and Mills were not close. Somehow Johnson could not connect with Mills as he had with others in Congress.

"He seemed intimidated by him," Kenny remarked. "Though I cannot imagine why."

The bill failed in the House in no small measure because of Wilbur Mills's opposition. It was one of the few times in those early years that the "Johnson Treatment" had failed him.

"Nevertheless," Kenny said, "it was a remarkable year of accomplishment given all he was facing. And now he faced getting himself elected in 1964."

Evans and Novak put it this way in their reporting of the legislative successes of Johnson:

> For the real difference in what Johnson did and what Kennedy probably would have done in the interminable 88th Congress was a matter of image—no trifling matter for the President of the United States. . . . Johnson's most significant legislative breakthrough was to establish an image in Congress, as with the public, of presidential mastery over Congress. He had cautiously hoarded his powers of majority leader to tame the Senate, and now he lustily expended the enormous powers of the presidency to tame Congress. And, in so doing, he strengthened his presidency.

Over dinner one night at Paul Young's restaurant, Kenny told Bobby that he believed that Johnson would be able to take much of the Kennedy agenda and get it done. "I think he will expand it beyond what you and I can imagine at this point. I know had your brother lived he would have done the same, but if Johnson can master the powers of the presidency the way he did the Senate, that is a good thing. It is also a good thing if we can get Humphrey in there as vice president to make sure he stays the course."

Bobby, who was then seriously looking at the Senate, but had not decided anything for sure, listened quietly to Kenny.

He seemed to measure his words carefully when he finally spoke.

"I agree with you pretty much, Kenny, but I have some concerns that I think can be watched carefully if we can get him to keep Nick Katzenbach in place. But I am concerned on the foreign policy front. Specifically, on Vietnam. I am worried. I know he is not focused on that just now, but much was left unfinished and unclear. I worry about the direction in which he will move."

Kenny sat in silence for a moment and then said, "Well, you are probably right, but he is a good man with the right instincts, who wants to do the right thing. I suggest that you need to stay engaged if you want to keep things moving in the right direction. After all, Bobby, you are our best hope going forward. We need you. The party needs you and so does your country."

Bobby smiled that sad, slightly haunted grin and said, "Yeah, you are just saying that, because you want me to pay for dinner."

The friends laughed.

The reality was that both men were at this stage unsure of their own futures. They would stay with Johnson to see him elected in his own right in 1964. Bobby would eventually decide on the Senate in New York; and Kenny would return to Massachusetts and run for governor. Larry O'Brien alone would stay on with Johnson.

EPILOGUE

Lyndon Johnson's presidency and policies changed the social fabric of America in many ways that we are all now familiar with and perhaps take for granted. However, his legacy will be forever divided between the Great Society programs that changed the lives of so many Americans and the Vietnam War, which divided the country, overtook his presidency, and killed so many in a senseless war.

Evans and Novak would report shortly after Johnson's successful election that "with his election in his own right Johnson was regaining his full physical vigor. Once again *The Treatment* was being administered—to intimate groups around his desk, to large groups in the East Room. For example, once, shortly after his Inauguration, every member of Congress was invited to the East Room in two shifts, on February 24 and 25, nominally to hear Vice President Hubert Humphrey's report on his trip to the Far East. But it was the president who popped up to take over and field the questions in his old bantering form from his Senate days."

Once in office under his own right, they reported that "Johnson further stretched and refined the new dimensions the powers of an office inherently more powerful than any in the world." Gone was the cautious, careful Johnson of the Kennedy years.

Generally speaking, the power of Lyndon Johnson had been well used for public purpose. Bob Novak and Rowland Evans wrote of Johnson:

> His Senate had censured Joseph McCarthy, passed the first civil rights act since reconstruction, and subdued a brief but concentrated assault on the Supreme Court by the reactionaries. His presidency had thus far wielded together a national consensus at an hour of strife and sorrow, he had tamed Congress to produce a vast outpouring of legislation that would change the social fabric of the nation for the better, he had lifted up those in need and provided a social safety net for those who fell along the way, and he presided over unprecedented economic prosperity . . . but Vietnam was none of these and his inflexibility would allow the war to overtake much of the dreams and hopes he had harbored when he first took office.

Kenny recalled: "Bobby told me a story once. I was up in Massachusetts by then, but Bobby had a meeting with Johnson over some issue, but not about Vietnam. He said, though, all Johnson talked about was Vietnam. He even took Bobby into a room where a map was laid out and showed Bobby what company was doing what with such and such a hill, and so forth."

Bobby said, "We never discussed what I went there to talk about. Vietnam seems to be consuming him. He was involved in the minutiae of the war in a manner that I thought did not bode well for the future."

Kenny said, "This was early days for Bobby in the Senate. It would take some time for him to forcefully take on Johnson, but Bobby told me after this meeting, he said, 'Kenny . . . the break over this war, when it comes, is inevitable . . . though right now I do not believe it would be helpful . . . but it is inevitable.' I was quiet for a moment. Then I said what I believed to be true, maybe I should not have, but I said it. 'The break was and is always going to happen, Bobby, because your time is coming and nobody can stop it. He, Johnson, probably knows that and understands it better than anyone.' Bobby didn't really reply. It would be a while before he was completely comfortable stepping away, but never out, from his brother's shadow."

The truth was from the time he got elected to the United Senate in November 1964, "Bobby Kennedy became the hope for the future to New Frontiersmen who counted the days to a Kennedy restoration." So wrote Rowland Evans and Bob Novak shortly after the election in a column that sent Lyndon Johnson through the roof. The words encapsulated all of Johnson's worst fears about Bobby Kennedy.

But at that time, Bobby had no real desire to openly break with the Johnson administration or risk a personal battle with Johnson. Though Bobby made clear that he did "consider himself as the preserver of John F. Kennedy's legacy and that Kennedy mystique."

"Beginning in 1965," Kenny explained, "Bobby, though careful, did begin to criticize and take issue with Johnson's foreign policy. For example, among other issues, he objected to the Dominican Republic intervention, felt that Johnson was not pushing hard enough on nuclear disarmament as his brother had. And with a trip to South America in late 1965, he gave the distinct impression that Johnson was not adhering to the true meaning of his brother's Alliance for Progress."

His steps were tentative and cautious. Bob Novak said, "On the central issue of Vietnam, Bobby held views critical of Johnson, but mostly kept it to himself. He also stayed aloof from the Peace Bloc in the Senate." It would be a long and painful process for Bobby to break outwardly with Johnson, but Johnson for one believed it was always going to come to pass.

"He cannot help himself, but take issue with anything I do," Johnson complained to Kenny shortly before Kenny left the White House.

Kenny had been opposed to the Vietnam War from the start and had told John Kennedy as much in a heated discussion in 1962. Kenny believed firmly in John Kennedy's last conversation with him on Vietnam when President Kennedy had told him: "Once I win in November, one of my first steps is to get us the hell out of Vietnam. I see no way that we can win in such a war." But, Johnson did not share that view and, moreover, was prone to listen to the military.

"Johnson," Kenny said, "unfortunately did not share John Kennedy's cynicism of the military and their promises. President Kennedy had learned the hard way in the first Cuba situation not to take the military at their word. He had learned to question their promises. As much as he respected McNamara—and he did—he also understood that it was important to keep him on a short leash in terms of these issues. Of course, this was Johnson's presidency, not Kennedy's, and so perhaps it is unfair of me to make such comparisons."

But despite Kenny's own opposition to the war, he did not stop his oldest son, Kenneth Jr., from going. Kenny felt he could not.

"Others have no choice, who am I to ask my son to do something less than honorable?" he explained. "I wouldn't, I would go if I were he; he knew that and he followed his sense of honor."

But Bobby Kennedy, despite personal reservations, was not ready to publicly oppose Johnson—not yet anyway. Novak reported that despite Bobby's personal opposition to the war, and while he had an aide who regularly attended meetings of the Peace Bloc in the Senate, Bobby remained quiet: "He declined an invitation to sign the Hartke letter attacking resumption of bombing . . . Kennedy instead issued a statement that was equivocal as to whether the bombing should have resumed, but suggested bombing North Vietnam would never win the war. Kennedy's uncharacteristic reticence resulted from his refusal (at this time) to split the Democratic Party and, indeed, the entire nation, into Johnson and Kennedy wings over so critical an issue as Vietnam. Yet, Bobby Kennedy was no man to keep quiet indefinitely on the great issues of the day."

The day would come, Kenny declared, when the break between Johnson and Kennedy over Vietnam was inevitable. Bobby chose the path he chose, to challenge Johnson not for some personal, ego-driven purpose, but rather because he knew he had to stop the war raging in Vietnam, the war raging in our cities, and he was the one to bring the country together.

Kenny recalled the last time he and Bobby spoke:

> He had just won California, and he said to me, shortly before going down to give his acceptance speech, "Kenny, do you think I am doing the right things? Dividing the party and maybe the country like this?"
>
> I said to him, and I meant what I said: "Bobby, you are the only man who can bring this country together and change the direction in which we are going. You are the only man who can bring blacks and whites together, and the only man who can stop this awful war and save our country."

There was a moment of silence and then in typical Bobby fashion, he said, "Well, gosh, when you put it that way."

> We both laughed.
> He then said, "Thanks, Kenny."
> We hung up. I never spoke to him again.

"The presidency has made every man who occupied it, no matter how small, bigger than he was; and no matter how big, not big enough for the job."

—*Lyndon B. Johnson*

ACKNOWLEDGMENTS

Special thanks to my great agent, the very classy Marcy Posner at Folio Literary Management, who stepped into this project midway and whose help and encouragement were essential to a successful completion.

Thanks as well to my editor Jon Arlan, whose enthusiasm, patience, and guidance were critical to this book. He really stepped up to the plate and helped get this book done. He is the kind of advocate and editor that writers love to work with.

Thanks as well to Skyhorse Publishing for their patience and determination to hang in there throughout the writing of this book.

Special thanks to Sander Vanocur for his remarkable interviews with my father. He has unmatched interview skills that have allowed us a rare look behind the scenes into history.

Thank you to Chris Matthews for his unwavering support and encouragement for this book and his help getting these stories told.

Thank you to John A. Farrell for his support and enthusiasm for these stories.

Thank you to my sister Kathleen for her remarkable, unwavering support and deeply shared passion in telling our father's story, his love for Jack and Bobby Kennedy, and especially this country.

A special thank you to the outstanding Ann Terry and the truly remarkable staff at the Hotel Harrington in Washington, DC. Without their unfailing support and encouragement this book would not have been possible.

Thank you to John Boyle, Eddie Braman, Richard Ronollo, and the terrific staff at Harry's Bar at the Hotel Harrington for keeping me well fed with lots of their great burgers, plenty of Diet Cokes, and encouragement.

As always, a special thank you to the fantastic Laurie Austin, now at the Harry S. Truman Presidential Library and Museum. She is always going above and beyond!

And, a special thank you to Maryrose Grossman and the terrific audio visual staff at the John F. Kennedy Presidential Library and Museum in Boston, Massachusetts.

Thank you to Barbara Cline at the Lyndon Baines Johnson Library and Museum in Austin, Texas. She was lovely. I look forward to working with her on future projects.

Thank you to the wonderful Rob Swan, Louis Montefusco, Kirk Eklund, and the other terrific supporters of the Kenneth P. O'Donnell Fund. Their friendship and support helped at such critical times along the way.

A very special thank you to Alice Hawa Koker, Sabrina Barnes, Marian Sliwinski, Yolanda Delgado, and Sergio and Nadim Anthony for their consistent support and in our shared memory of our beloved Eunice and of course Tiger Baby—they were there throughout all of the ups and downs of this remarkable journey.

Finally, in this difficult political time for our country and indeed the world, this book is dedicated to President John F. Kennedy, President Lyndon B. Johnson, Senator Robert F. Kennedy, and the founding members of the "Irish

Brotherhood"—Kenny O'Donnell and Larry O'Brien—who sacrificed so much for their firm and unwavering belief in the importance of the institutions and the people that make this remarkable democracy vital to mankind.

It seems appropriate, now more than ever, to share the words of President Abraham Lincoln, whom my father so admired:

> Fellow-citizens, we cannot escape history. We of this Congress and this administration, will be remembered in spite of ourselves. No personal significance, or insignificance, can spare one or another of us. The fiery trial through which we pass, will light us down, in honor or dishonor, to the latest generation. The world knows we do know how to save it. We—even we here—hold the power, and bear the responsibility. In giving freedom to the slave, we assure freedom to the free—honorable alike in what we give, and what we preserve. We shall nobly save, or meanly lose, the last best hope of earth. Other means may succeed; this could not fail. The way is plain, peaceful, generous, just—a way which, if followed, the world will forever applaud, and God must forever bless. (Washington, DC, December 1, 1862)

SOURCES

The primary sources consulted in researching this book include:

The Kenneth P. O'Donnell Oral History Interviews, Tapes, and Notes. The Kenneth P. O'Donnell Private Collection.

The A. Justine O'Donnell Oral History and Notes. The Kenneth P. O'Donnell Private Collection.

The Cleo O'Donnell Oral History Interview. Private Collection.

Angie Novello Interview and Oral History. The Kenneth P. O'Donnell Private Collection.

The Robert F. Kennedy Oral History Interview. John F. Kennedy Library and Museum, Boston.

Lady Bird Johnson Oral History Interview. Lyndon Baines Johnson Library and Museum, Austin.

Walter Jenkins Oral History Interview. Lyndon Baines Johnson Library and Museum, Austin.

In addition to the oral histories, interviews, and tapes mentioned above, other sources consulted include:

Califano, Joseph A. Jr. *The Triumph & Tragedy of Lyndon Johnson: The White House Years.* New York: Simon & Schuster, 2015.

Caro, Robert A. *The Passage of Power: The Years of Lyndon Johnson.* New York: Knopf, 2013.

Dallek, Robert. *An Unfinished Life: John F. Kennedy, 1917–1963.* New York: Little Brown & Company, 2003.

Evans, Rowland and Robert Novak. *Lyndon B. Johnson: The Exercise of Power.* New American Library, 1966.

_____. Columns and interviews from day-to-day reporting, 1958 to 1965.

Goodwin, Doris Kearns. *Lyndon Johnson and the American Dream.* New York: Harper & Row, 1976.

Matthews, Chris. *Jack Kennedy: Elusive Hero.* New York: Simon & Schuster, 2011.

_____. *Bobby Kennedy: Raging Spirit.* New York: Simon & Schuster, 2017.

O'Donnell, Helen. *A Common Good: The Friendship of Robert F. Kennedy and Kenneth P. O'Donnell,* book and unpublished interviews and notes. New York: William Morrow, 1998.

_____. *The Irish Brotherhood: John F. Kennedy, His Inner Circle and the Improbable Rise to the Presidency,* book and unpublished interviews and notes. Berkley: Counterpoint, 2015.

Photographs courtesy of:
The John F. Kennedy Library and Museum, Boston.
The Lyndon Baines Johnson Library and Museum, Austin.
The Associated Press.